6148

ONE VOICE, MANY RHYTHMS

A SERIES OF REFLECTIONS FOR PASTORAL AGENTS
ON THE ROLE OF LITURGY, SPIRITUALITY,
AND POPULAR PIETY IN THE CULTURALLY DIVERSE
ASSEMBLIES OF THE UNITED STATES

Juan J. Sosa

PASTORAL
PRESS
PORTLAND · OREGON

One Voice, Many Rhythms
JUAN J. SOSA

ISBN 978-1-56929-080-4

© 2008 Pastoral Press. All rights reserved.
An imprint of OCP
5536 NE Hassalo
Portland, OR 97213-3638
Phone: 1-800-LITURGY (548-8749)
E-mail: liturgy@ocp.org
Web: ocp.org

Publisher: John J. Limb
Director of Editorial Processes: Eric Schumock
Director of Artist Relations & Product Development: Tom Tomaszek
Editor: Bari Colombari
Editing Assistance: Mónica Rodríguez
Book Layout: Melissa Schmidt
Art Direction: Judy Urben
Cover Art: Rogelio Zelada

Printed in the United States of America

FATHER JUAN J. SOSA

Dedication

I dedicate this work to the members of the *Instituto Nacional Hispano de Liturgia*, who, since 1979, have nourished me and encouraged me to nourish others, especially in our Hispanic Catholic assemblies, in the love and knowledge of the liturgy of the Latin Rite of the Catholic Church.

TABLE OF CONTENTS

FOREWORD

At the heart of this book by Father Juan Sosa, my friend and colleague at the Instituto de Liturgia Hispana for many years, is the theme of popular religion. Father Sosa is one of the leading Hispanic pastoralists who has studied, reflected, written, and taught on this very important aspect of the faith of many people who make up the universal Church.

The other prevailing theme of this book is that of ministry in a multicultural setting. It is important to consider both themes together. Many cultures have brought their traditions and faith expressions to our Church and have added to the richness of the tapestry of Catholicism in the United States.

Popular religion and another related theme, the inculturation of the Gospel, have received much attention in the teachings of the Church since the Second Vatican Council. The *Constitution on the Sacred Liturgy* (*Sacrosanctum Concilium*) refers to the possibility of adapting the Roman liturgy to the various cultures of peoples: "Even in the liturgy, the Church has no wish to impose a rigid uniformity in matters which do not implicate the faith or the good of the whole community" (37). The *Dogmatic Constitution on the Church* (*Lumen Gentium*) speaks of the multiplicity of gifts and graces received by members of the people of God; the Church favors and assumes the riches and customs of all peoples and then "purifies, strengthens, elevates and ennobles them" (13).

In his often-quoted 1975 work, *Evangelii Nuntiandi* (*On Evangelization in the Modern World*), Pope Paul VI recognized the value of popular Catholicism. While warning against the possible excesses of popular religiosity, he nonetheless wrote about the values that often accompany these faith expressions. If well directed, he pointed out, popular piety manifests a thirst for God, makes people generous, and imbues the faithful with the spirit of sacrifice. It can lead to an acute awareness of God's attributes, like his "fatherhood, providence, [and] loving and constant presence" (48).

Each of the general conferences of the bishops of Latin America, beginning in Medellín, Colombia (1968), and later in Puebla, Mexico (1979); Santo Domingo, Dominican Republic (1992); and Aparecida, Brazil (2007), underscored the importance of popular religion.

I have been especially impressed by what the Latin American bishops said at their general conference in Puebla. "At its core, the religiosity of the people is a storehouse of values that offers the answers of Christian wisdom to the great questions of life. The Catholic wisdom of the common people is capable of fashioning a vital synthesis. It creatively combines the divine and the human, Christ and Mary, Spirit and body, communion and institution, person and community, faith and homeland, intelligence and emotion. This wisdom is a Christian humanism that radically affirms the dignity of every human person as a child of God, establishes a basic fraternity, teaches people how to encounter nature and understand work, and provides reasons for joy and humor even in the midst of a very hard life" (448).

In their 1994 pastoral letter on Hispanic ministry, *The Hispanic Presence: Challenge and Commitment*, the US bishops said that Hispanic spirituality is an example of how deeply Christianity can permeate the roots of a culture. The bishops went on to say that ecclesial life vibrant with a profound sense of the transcendent, such as is found in Hispanic popular Catholicism, can also be a remarkable witness to the more secularized members of our society (*cf.* subsection o on Popular Catholicism).

At the general conference of Latin American bishops in Aparecida, Pope Benedict XVI began his extended inaugural session talk by describing and affirming popular religion in Latin America. He described the way the Christian faith was accepted through the work of missionaries in Latin America. The indigenous peoples welcomed Christ, the unknown God, whom their ancestors were seeking, without realizing it, in their rich religious traditions. He said that "they received the Holy Spirit who came to make their cultures fruitful, purifying them and developing the numerous seeds that the incarnate Word had planted in them, thereby guiding them along the paths of the Gospel" (1).

The Holy Father referred to the synthesis between the cultures of the Americas and the Christian faith, as was done at Puebla in 1977. He said, "This religiosity is also expressed in devotion to the saints with their patronal feasts, in love for the Pope and other pastors and in love for the universal Church as a great family of God.... All this forms the great mosaic of popular piety which is the precious treasure of the Catholic Church in Latin America, and must be protected, promoted and, when necessary, purified" (1).

The Hispanic Church in the US is an extension, in many ways, of the Church in Latin America. Thus, whatever is said of the popular religion of the peoples of Latin America applies also to the Hispanics in the US. In this book, Father Sosa describes how Latin American piety is alive and well among Hispanic Catholics in North America.

One of the important dimensions of Hispanic spirituality to keep in mind is the way popular religious traditions keep people in touch with the spirituality of their ancestors. In the practice of this piety, there is a reaching back in time, as it were, to a tradition and history of faith. This practice happens in such a way that one's spirituality is more than an isolated individual or private experience; it is, for Hispanics, a people's legacy.

In conversations among the members of the Instituto de Liturgia Hispana, in which Father Sosa has had a prominent place, we have reflected on the world of the sacred among Hispanic people. There are, first of all, sacred persons. Jesus is the holiest person in whom the Hispanic popular spirituality centers its faith. Popular titles for Jesus in Spanish are *El Divino Salvador* (The Divine Savior), *Cristo Rey* (Christ the King), *El Niño Dios* (The God Child), and *El Señor de las Misericordias* (The Merciful Lord). Traditions centering on the person of Christ are celebrated most during Holy Week.

In the Hispanic tradition, the Blessed Virgin Mary is also an important figure. She is revered as the Mother of God and attributed divine qualities, like mercy, love, and majesty. A popular expression distinguishes Roman Catholics from those of other Christian denominations: "I believe in God and in Mary."

Every country in Latin America has a particular title for Mary that is often ingrained into its national and even patriotic spirit. In Mexico, she is Our Lady of Guadalupe (*Nuestra Señora de Guadalupe*); in Puerto Rico, Our Lady of Providence (*Nuestra Señora de la Providencia*). In Cuba, she is Our Lady of the Charity of El Cobre (*Nuestra Señora de la Caridad del Cobre*), and in the Dominican Republic, she is Our Lady of Mercies (*Nuestra Señora de las Mercedes*).

Saints are popular in the Hispanic tradition, not only as those who continue to hand on the faith and models to Hispanic devotees, but also as those who serve as sources of favors for those who believe in them. Their intercessory powers are immense in the religious thinking of Hispanics.

Sacred objects play a role as well and are seen more as magic or lucky charms. They are reminders and symbols of the ever-abiding presence of God, of his protection and providential care. They represent the transcendent, the world of the spirit, God's world and scheme of things.

In the popular religiosity of Latin America, there are even sacred events and times. Certain happenings signal God's entrance into the temporal human sphere. Events like Holy Week, the Christmas season (especially Christmas Eve), and a feast of the Virgin or of a saint (especially those pertaining to one's national origin) are times that call for special family and community gatherings, celebrations of a both religious and social nature. Moments of passage are special times and are celebrated as well. These include baptisms, first Communions, confirmations, *quinceañeras*, weddings, and funerals. They carry with them family and religious traditions and are times that call for a renewed commitment to Christian discipleship. They are also reminders of the Catholic tradition that must be maintained and handed on to future generations.

At this time in the history of the Church in the United States, we are increasingly aware of the importance of the gifts that are brought to us by cultures from all over the world. At the millennial celebration of our faith organized by the US bishops and held in Los Angeles in 2000, this multicultural dimension of the US Church was given merited attention. At the Encuentro Nacional Hispano, we heard one another's heroic stories of faith and how important it is for us to be reconciled to one another. It is interesting to note that, in the restructuring of the US Conference of Catholic Bishops (USCCB), one of the priorities centers on cultural diversity in the Church, with a special emphasis on Hispanic ministry in the spirit of Encuentro 2000.

Father Juan Sosa's work helps us in creating practical ways of accepting the challenge of reconciliation and the need for us to be a Church *in communio*. In fact, Father Sosa's insights and suggestions will help the entire Church deal with multicultural challenges in the areas of liturgical language, music, and catechesis. He calls us to consider the needed restructuring of our institutions, pastoral planning and, above all, a renewed commitment to work toward bringing one voice out of many rhythms—one voice in praise of the one God and Father of all.

Most Reverend Ricardo Ramírez, CSB
Bishop of Las Cruces, New Mexico

Introduction

At the turn of the second millennium and the twentieth century, I was asked to participate in a number of national and diocesan conferences in which the subject popularly known as multicultural worship was to be highlighted. I was delighted! A topic that had been the bread and butter of many dedicated pastoral agents—priests, deacons, catechists, musicians, and many other lay leaders—for so many decades and under strenuous pastoral circumstances was finally receiving attention at a wider national level.

As one of many speakers that have addressed this topic consistently in the classroom or at parish and diocesan gatherings over the last three decades, I felt at this time that, from a national platform, it was to reach a large number of dedicated lay ministers for whom the reason for the subject matter was not a priority at all. And it did reach them in New Orleans, Houston, Salt Lake City, Orlando, Seattle, Albuquerque, Chicago, Phoenix, Los Angeles, and New York. It had impact particularly in those urban centers that continue to witness the growth of Hispanic communities from Latin America together with the arrival of Catholic families from parts of India, Nigeria, the Philippines, Vietnam, and other sections of Asia. Whatever one could contribute to the understanding of multicultural church and worship was to become an aid to pastoral leaders who searched for ways in which to serve such culturally diverse assemblies, particularly in the areas of worship and spirituality.

However, I always asked myself after each conference, "Was this enough?" I knew that the efforts made by diocesan and/or national personnel aimed at reaching our pastoral leaders with this subject would only be the beginning, but it was a good beginning! Such became the intention of Encuentro and Mission 2000, the gathering called by the US bishops in Los Angeles, California, at the onset of a new millennium to address the collaboration of all pastoral agents in the area of evangelization to all cultures. Yet, while none of these efforts, I am sure, was meant to become a token expression of evangelization in the United States as in the expression "Okay, we've done that; let's now move on to another agenda item," in some areas and to some people it seems that it has.

Sadly enough, as I continue to visit some of these areas of the country through the Instituto Nacional Hispano de Liturgia, it appears that the implementation of the concepts and criteria that were shared and accepted for the most part unanimously during these gatherings has not been fully made. Some pastoral limitations have surfaced since the year 2000. Rather than exploring creative ways of expanding services to the culturally diverse people among us, financial restraints seemed to have impaired this expansion and have forced some of our shepherds to place the needs of all cultural groups under one general umbrella; consequently, a number of pastoral agents seem to perceive cultural diversity as the amalgamation of all cultures foreign to the mainstream culture of the United States; hence, the misconstrued perception behind the term "multicultural."

Like any other term, "multicultural" can be used in many ways and for many purposes—from recognizing the need of individual cultural groups to integrate into the larger society while keeping their unique identity at hand, to the need to put everyone together in the category of foreign minority, in the style of the long-forgotten melting pot/assimilationist theories of the twentieth century that gave birth to the term "minority." When I use the term "multicultural" in these reflections, I stand far away from the latter tendency and uphold the criteria that shape the concept of integration and that truly address the actual nature of the term.

For this reason, I have simply attempted to expand the marvelous efforts already displayed by many bishops, priests, deacons, and lay leaders of our Church by enhancing, though humbly, their reflections, lest we forget our focus on evangelization as Church in the United States and fall into the temptation of pastoral simplification or theological reductionism. Those who know me understand that I do not pretend to offer the final word on this pastoral topic. Rather, I strive to present a few more concepts and practical suggestions to the ongoing theological reflection that attempts to integrate the revealed word of God with our pastoral experience as Church in the United States and in the twenty-first century. Whereas most of these reflections emerge out of my involvement with the Instituto Nacional Hispano de Liturgia, I believe that many of the principles of criteria exposed throughout may apply to many other faith communities in our country.

I have attempted to collect some of the concepts and experiences that I shared with hundreds of participants in the late 1990s and early years of the twenty-first century on subjects that range from multicultural worship to the spirituality of pastoral musicians. To accomplish this task, I have shared some of my personal experiences. I also hope to have placed these reflections in a certain logical order, at least logical to me, from the general concepts and criteria to the more specific exhortations and applications to our pastoral agents.

In the first two reflections I lay out the ingredients to become multicultural by pointing out that, as a Church, we are called by Jesus to become a bridge unto others, and by analyzing the anthropological components of being multicultural. The next articles address the spirituality that our Hispanic Catholics bring to their integration into the larger community, primarily the love of popular piety, transmitted at home, and the love of the Eucharist, discovered in Church. In this context, I begin to unveil the work of the Instituto throughout the United States, particularly the *Ordo Missae* study of 1982 and its results. The next essays flow from the results of this study and the priorities set forth by those who partici- pated in it: liturgical music, liturgical texts, and ministries (i.e., catechists and musicians, many times exercised by the same dedicated person for the same community without too many resources). I left out the element of liturgical gesture because it applies more to specific subcultures within the larger Latino community and because it should be evident from my reflections on symbols and symbolic language.

As I developed each reflection, I tried to avoid repeating concepts or ideas already expressed in previous reflections, although I must admit that we can benefit from a bit of repetition when dealing with this subject matter. In some cases, repetition became unavoidable due to the content of the specific essay or conference and the specific circumstances in which it was delivered. At the onset, moreover, allow me to share two of the basic principles that have served to guide me in these reflections:

- From an anthropological perspective: cultural diversity in urban soci- eties is ruled by the principle of integration that encourages people to get in touch with their cultural roots while contributing effectively to the larger society. Without these roots, without any references to that worldview of myths and symbols in which one has grown and has learned to live, the individual can barely survive in such a complex soci- ety as ours, a society deprived of myths and symbols that is generally oriented to scientific and material successes. Cultural diversity seems to be more difficult in rural societies that, by nature, resist changes and/or innovations and do not make much room for outsiders.

- From a theological perspective: liturgical celebrations cannot be sepa- rated from sound theological reflections, lest such celebrations fall into either rubricism (strictly external and repetitive) on one side and rela- tivism (anything goes) and/or magical forms of ritual (superstitions) on the other. We must understand the why of what we celebrate before we apply the how of any celebration. The why lies in the faith-filled awareness of the Paschal Mystery of Jesus Christ ever present in our midst that gathers us as an assembly of believers who share one Lord, one faith, and one baptism. Hence, the ecclesiology (being Church) of each community (diocese or parish) antecedes the mechanisms of their multicultural worship.

Undoubtedly, the Eucharist gathers us each week to celebrate the Paschal Mystery; the Eucharist allows us to offer our lives to the Father in and with Jesus Christ, who surrendered himself on the Cross to teach us how to love and serve others. In the spirit of the Year of the Eucharist (October 2004–October 2005), convoked by the late Pope John Paul II and concluded by Pope Benedict XVI, these reflections, in their most humble ambitions, merely wish to echo, among other exhortations, Saint Paul:

> Scripture says: "No one who believes in him will be put to shame." Here there is no difference between Jew and Greek; all have the same Lord, rich in mercy toward all who call upon him. "Everyone who calls on the name of the Lord will be saved." But how shall they call on him in whom they have not believed? And how can they believe unless they have heard of him? And how can they hear unless there is someone to preach? And how can men preach unless they are sent? Scripture says, "How beautiful are the feet of those who announce good news" (Romans 10:11–15).

BUILDING BRIDGES AS WE PRAY
What does it mean to be Church in a multicultural society?

The following reflections were offered as a keynote talk at the Orlando Liturgical Conference that took place on September 18–20, 1997. At that time, I was serving as executive director of ministry of worship and spiritual life in the Archdiocese of Miami, Florida.

There is a favorite side of worship that I seem to enjoy more and more as the years go by. I am referring to that field that I call liturgical bloopers. I am sure that all of us have experienced it at some time or another.

Liturgical bloopers surface at unexpected moments of ritual to surprise us, sometimes to depress us and, for sure, most of the time, to make us angry. As a master of ceremonies for pontifical celebrations in Miami and other places, I have witnessed many of them. For reasons unknown to me, liturgical bloopers become more evident when distinguished members of the hierarchy preside at these celebrations. I recall occasions such as a reader announcing with excitement "The Letter to the Philippines" and then proceeding to read the wrong verses; sacristans forgetting the lemon, bread, and soap to wash the hands of the prelate after the rite of anointing at confirmation; and deacons dropping lit charcoal on the carpet before the actual incensation of the bishop. These, of course, I call pontifical bloopers.

Most of us have survived similar occurrences in our parish. In parishes, liturgical bloopers range from that common scene in which the neophyte altar server brings the deacon or priest water instead of wine, to witnessing a celebrant at Mass remember, during the elevation of the host, that he needs wine and water in the chalice. Others have skipped from the Holy, Holy, Holy to the Our Father (obviously, having to rewind their enthusiasm to the eucharistic prayer). Some have heard of an extraordinary minister of holy Communion who returned to the credence table to pour wine from the cruets into the cup that holds the precious blood because "it was running out and the line was too long." At this point, some would consider the blooper an abuse.

I know, of course, that some liturgical bloopers are more serious than others. And with all due reverence to the sacredness of Catholic ritual, while it is evident that irritation emerges out of these brief, yet pictorial, experiences when we see others perform them, no liturgical blooper lies more heavily on one's heart than the one for which one is personally responsible. I am sure all of us can remember at least one in which we have been involved or for which we are responsible.

It was the solemnity of Saints Peter and Paul, great martyrs of the Church, held on a Sunday that year. I participated at the entrance procession for Sunday Eucharist at Miami's cathedral wearing white vestments. Not until the responsorial psalm did I become aware of this unthinkable faux pas. What is Father to do? The only option was to wait until the presentation of the gifts, at which time I received the bread and wine, walked to the credenza, slightly hidden from the assembly, and changed my vestments from white to red with the kind assistance of a sacristan who had been summoned to help.

What amazed me the most about this incident was the fact that no one noticed the difference, and maybe no one seemed to care. This brings me to my original thought of why I seem to enjoy liturgical bloopers: while they surface from unintentional—sometimes disconnected—minds and bodies, they manifest how little we are in actual control of the worship experience once it has started. We celebrants, deacons, readers, musicians, cantors, ushers, altar servers, sacristans, and extraordinary ministers of holy Communion do not run the liturgy; we are not in control. Someone greater than us runs it. God is at the center of our celebrations and we, fragile and disconnected as we at times appear to be, are at his service; we are his instruments. What do I learn from these experiences? One word describes it the best: *relax*!

Each time any of these bloopers hits a parish celebration, once we have done our best, we can do very little else. We need to learn to enjoy them and not be mortified by their existence. We need to learn to relax, for through these bloopers, the Lord seems to tell us every so often in our worship experience, "Don't get too angry, too depressed, or too dejected, for I am with you and I love you, bloopers or not."

Relax is the first of four words beginning with *R* that I would like to share with you as we reflect together on our topic: building bridges as we pray, building bridges between the cultural communities that constitute our parish families in the Church of the United States.

There has been a long-standing joke among some of our priests in Miami: "Please pray that Brazil may not suffer a coup d'etat or Brazilians will be coming over here by the thousands and we'll have to learn a new language." I used to smile then and I still smile now at this seemingly helpless petition because we have thousands of Brazilians in South Florida and there has been no significant coup d'etat in that country. In fact, the Archbishop just assigned two Brazilian-born priests of the Scalabrinian community as director and assistant to that apostolate, and they have established four centers to minister to the Brazilians in Portuguese.

"Relax," I say to those who grow weary. God never permits complex situations to appear without also providing the gifts to deal with them. I am sure that you, too, have become aware of the complexity of human life, of the diversity of Catholic groups that continue to grow in our parish communities. Two key questions may continually surface in your mind: "Do we have to learn all of their languages?" and "How do we cope with them?"

"Relax," I say to you. You do not have to learn all of their languages, although knowing one more language at least would be nice, for language is the doorway to the culture of others. But often there's a lack of time or resources, so as pastoral agents committed to evangelization we need to learn the faith symbols embedded in their culture; if language is the vehicle to culture, symbols form the gateway to the heart, and the heart is our business. I say to you, "Relax," because in this area we have more in common with the many diverse groups that knock on the doors of our parishes and schools than we want to admit.

We share a Catholic heritage and a rich tradition of symbolic language that we cannot ignore and that we must continue to explore inside the liturgy as well as outside it. This, I propose to you, is the most important element for us to begin to build bridges with, more than the language of the culture itself. However, do not think I am only referring to water and oil, images of Mary and the saints, or music and gestures as symbols. We, as an assembly, are also ministerial symbols to one another. Individually and as a family, we first need to show that we care, that we are open to other groups regardless of the languages they speak. We need to show that we care enough to want to know about them and their culture because we want to worship with them, even if they worship separately when they assemble. We, with our physical presence above all, constitute a symbol of hospitality that is more eloquent than the languages of the world. We can choose to communicate to others that they belong to the rest of the faithful in this community of faith, or that they do not belong and that they will remain strangers and foreigners.

We need to learn from Jesus. To him, a Roman centurion was no different from a Samaritan woman, a Galilean fisherman, or a Canaanite woman. He welcomed all into his heart and invited them to belong to the kingdom. He was physically present to them first, before he spoke to them, for he was the Word. The Church, in the name of Jesus, has always been present to a complex world in which social standards and family needs have clashed through the centuries. Through the Gospel texts, Jesus assures us, "Relax!"

If our hearts have been enriched by Christ's presence, then we can welcome all who wish to join us at worship. To do so we need to develop our second *R*, "respect."

The need to learn to respect others and their differences emerges out of our own acceptance of diversity itself as a necessary criterion for building bridges with them. Often it is particularly challenging for us to accept others.

We are the founding families, the priestly leadership of the parish community. We are the principals and teachers of the schools or parish programs. Our challenge is to accept in others—strangers to our ways, or new arrivals—new gifts and new ways of seeing and expressing reality that can enrich our own gifts. Yet respect is based on this acceptance of diversity as a gift from God. It is for the good of all, and is not a threat!

At the root of the word "diversity" and its interpretation, however, are two different philosophical positions. One has been called realism, the other moderate realism. I have often witnessed the first in the words and actions of many of our long-standing and founding parishioners. Extreme realism, some claim, places individuals as receptive vessels of all reality. In simple words: "I have been born here, my family has given me this vision, and my country has taught me how to deal with others. I see the world like this because I perceive it through my senses like this. I am, therefore, right and everyone else is not. My perception of reality does not allow me to admit another perception equal to mine; mine is better, they are wrong. In other words, my perspective and my interpretation of reality is the best. All other ways are inferior to mine."

Whereas this philosophical position gives birth to a cultural attitude in which diversity has no place, moderate realism provides us with an alternative attitude. Moderate realism indicates that individuals interact as seekers of reality, not as problem-solvers, as people who look for the mystery of life in themselves and their communities, as people who appear to grow always in search of the truth. They accept the fact that they can perceive only part of reality and, more significantly, can accept other people's perceptions and expressions of reality, even if these perspectives differ from their own. They do not need to change or water down their own perception of reality, yet they remain open to dialogue with others about their perception. Of course, they can disagree with them on various issues, but most of the time they are enriched by them, even in their disagreement.

The acceptance of diversity, then, as a viable option among cultural groups makes the term "cultural pluralism" a bit clearer. The US bishops seem to affirm it, as their document "Cultural Pluralism in the United States" (January 1981) indicates.[1]

For us to celebrate diversity in our unity, we need to respect one another in the uniqueness of our diversity. We live in a social milieu that calls for pluralism and not uniformity. Our religious heritage is marked not only by a consistent presence of cultural pluralism, but also theological pluralism, which should not threaten anyone. The presence of so many cultural Catholic groups in our country and in our parishes calls for the need to address diversity at diocesan and local levels in prophetic and creative ways.

We can build bridges at prayer by celebrating our diversity, but before the actual celebration takes place, we need to address those issues outside the liturgical environment that affects us in our specific setting. We need to follow up that well-known liturgical principle that addresses community prayer as the expression of the actual community assembled at prayer. Several faith communities seem to have accomplished this task by dealing with diversity at staff meetings, liturgy committee meetings, and parish assemblies because they are willing to answer, with specific data, the basic liturgical questions: Who are we, the assembly called and gathered to celebrate? Do we all share the same sense of belonging? These questions need to be addressed before proceeding to prepare the actual celebrations at a cathedral level or in a parish setting.

Many continue to experience and express the richness of diversity at key moments of the liturgical year through good multicultural celebrations, e.g., Thanksgiving, Christmas, the Paschal Triduum, Pentecost, and parish anniversaries. These are occasions when communities need to experience themselves more closely linked to the mystery of Christ as expressed in the unity of faith. These times need excellent planning, involving readers of different language texts, printed programs that are not repetitive, creative expression of the intercessions and, best of all, music that is appealing to all. They cannot become major celebrations in which the groups are represented by token improvisations with a sprinkling of cultural symbols. To plan such multicultural moments, the text of the bishops' document on cultural pluralism can guide the preparers of the liturgy. Preparers can also consult one or two good articles on inculturation or simply a reflective dialogue on chapters 1 and 2 of the Acts of the Apostles. These various resources can guide the group in processing ways by which they can learn to channel their diversity while expressing their unity, as Saint Paul would say, in one Lord, one faith and one baptism (Ephesians 4:5).[2]

At the level of Sunday assembly, several other communities have begun to reflect respect for diversity by making adequate adaptations of the introductory rite of the eucharistic celebration. This does not mean a ten-minute homily by the presider but, rather, a more creative involvement of those present. Very often the brief, though consistent, introduction of new members of the community before Mass begins, or the simple greeting of one another with a handshake, can begin to break down old images and fears brought about by a narrow view of culture and faith. There are ways to achieve these things since God has never given his instruments a complex reality without the gifts to deal with it. We just need to discover those gifts in the community. To do so, we need to reach out beyond our comfortable standards and projects to experience the stranger in his or her search to belong.

An authentic respect for diversity, born of a prayerful attitude that surfaces when we relax in the Lord, leads us to our third *R*, "rejoice." Frankly, we rejoice when we grow in our awareness that we are continuing in our local Church the Pentecost experience of Acts, not the Tower of Babel of Genesis. If we can relax with the God who humors us in many unexpected ways, and if we can recognize the presence of Jesus in others to such a degree that we can learn to respect them as unique gifts to the community, then we can rejoice as the apostles did when they experienced Pentecost:

> "We are Parthians, Medes, and Elamites, inhabitants of Mesopotamia, Judea and Cappadocia, Pontus and Asia, Phrygia and Pamphylia, Egypt and the districts of Libya near Cyrene, as well as travelers from Rome, both Jews and converts to Judaism, Cretans and Arabs, yet we hear them speaking in our own tongues of the mighty acts of God." They were all astounded and bewildered, and said to one another, "What does this mean?" But others said, scoffing, "They have had too much new wine!" (Acts of the Apostles 2:9–13, *New American Bible*)

Rejoice, but do not have too much wine! The Pentecost experience is a joyful and confusing experience by which God's mystery is revealed to each of us, empowering us to do more than we can humanly handle. It is the experience of God's Holy Spirit in our lives. And who has not witnessed this experience in ministry?

We can rejoice when we are not overwhelmed by stress or exhaustion and when we are not overtaken by needless worries or tensions. We can rejoice when we are free to let go instead of to control, when we see others grow and take our place in the ministry, and when we can take the time to listen to one another as persons instead of listening to one another only as part of our tasks. We can rejoice when we stop focusing on problems and begin to focus on possibilities that, with the support of others, can take root and develop. If we only focus on problems, nothing will happen, or we will become a problem to others, to ourselves, and to the Church.

Rejoicing obviously comes from a mature spirituality that is constantly nourished by prayer, diversity in human relationships, and creative nourishment. It does not merely happen; one must work at it.

Let us consider three areas briefly: prayer, diversity in human relationships, and creative nourishment. Through personal prayer, besides formal prayer, I find myself more often committed to face my own feelings (even if at times they seem to be a bit ugly) and to tell God about them. It might be after a meeting or while I am driving, or just in my own space, but I feel very honest afterwards. This is a gift of prayer.

It is a gift of diversity in human relationships that I find myself calling people who have enriched me in the past, or are enriching me now. I find myself breaking out of my routine—the routines all of us tend to get into after a certain age—and working at meeting others outside of my routine.

Creative nourishment is truly a gift. I love the arts in general and I need the arts in my life for nourishment and expression, yet I find myself choosier about what area of the arts I should explore. First, being involved with the arts, at least here in America, is an expensive proposition and, second, not all that is presented as artistic is good. Good movies have always been part of my creative nourishment. I recommend two wonderful movies that explore the area of redemption through facing oneself and overcoming one's foibles. They are also both wonderful sources of entertainment, as well as wonderful subjects for group dialogue. Although they are known as foreign films, they hit home in special ways. One is *Kolya*, a Czech film that describes the relationship between an egotistical man and a child who frees him from his own self-centeredness. The other production, the wonderfully crafted Japanese film *Shall We Dance*, cries out to people of all ages and cultures to be open to growth and transformation through ongoing human interaction, represented in the film through dancing.

I have found myself rejoicing more in my prayer, in my relationships, and in my overall ministry and I have been able to show more rejoicing than stress in my work. I am working at focusing more on people than on the problems that the ministry places before me. Allow me to reiterate it through an old expression: "Try it, you'll like it!"

We now have arrived at the last *R*, "restore." Building bridges as we pray involves ministers who not only experience redemption or healing in their lives, but are committed to facilitating it for others. To live out our commitment in a multicultural setting without unnecessary frustrations, we must dare to look into the hearts of others with inquisitive eyes.

It is known that the experience of immigration may bring about fragmentation in most families. New social strains appear in the lives of the immigrant families when they arrive to participate in a larger, more dominant society. These strains become stressful experiences, and they usually appear in three key areas: the economic level, the social level, and the meaning level.

Out of these three areas, the meaning level, where the faith experience of the family members lies, usually suffers the most. Family members become preoccupied with solving their economic situation at the risk of disorganizing themselves socially. Lawyers and doctors in one culture find themselves as short order cooks, gas station attendants, or dishwashers in our own. The change in their social status tends to decrease a certain level of prestige in the family that only time and hard work can help heal. In many cases, this reversal of social status places undue pressure on the children who are now expected to always succeed where their parents could not. By the same token, were they to turn to their faith community first they would find enough support at the meaning level, but they usually do not until a major crisis arises in their lives and in the lives of those with whom they share this new experience. By that time, it may be too late. Where faith and Church were significant elements in the life of a family in their country of origin, in this country they may find it too complex and quite unreachable. We must respond as Church leaders to this unique situation, more frequent in our communities as the years pass.

I propose to you that we, as pastoral agents, must be fully aware of the many crises that our cultural groups experience as they come before us in our rectories or schools. While we need to attend to and alleviate the economic or family crises, we also need to address the spiritual crises that may assume different features for them. They may not understand the concept of Church that requires registration forms, envelopes, and stewardship to praise God. They may be challenged by the concepts of waiting lists to get a child enrolled in a parish school or having to make an appointment with a person who can understand and guide them through a new setting. Their challenges are now, but the appointment is in the future.

I also propose to you that we, as pastoral agents, can only help alleviate these crises when we take the time to look beyond the surface of those with whom we come in contact to seek out what truly lies in their hearts as they search for a new beginning. The process of restoration for us, as well as for all entrusted to our care, comes from healing the disintegration of the meaning level and not just from attempting to solve the crises brought about by the other social strains. After all, are we not called to share in the healing and restoring ministry of Jesus as members of the Church and, especially, as his instruments? Here is our choice, either to treat one another as tourists, only from the superficial level of appearances, or to engage in a growing spiritual dialogue that makes us all pilgrims on the same journey as we strive to know one another, heart to heart.

These are four *R*s that constitute this pilgrimage: "relaxation" in the Lord who sees us with his heart and knows how hard we try. Authentic "respect" for others that allows us to accept and maintain diversity while bringing many into the unity of our ecclesial family. The ability to "rejoice" in and with him who faced the multicultural aspects of the kingdom before we ever did and whose Spirit never fails us. Finally, the commitment to "restore" others in their search for meaning and faith, particularly when most of them seem to experience a drastic disintegration of their family and spiritual values.

As an illustration, I'd like to share a personal experience. It was my first time in the Holy Land. My priest friend and I decided to walk the streets of old Jerusalem early in the morning, seeking a Catholic church for worship. The streets were empty and the shops were closed. Only two children seemed to roam around the narrow alleys. They spotted us, however, and proceeded to approach us. We did not know any Arabic and they did not know English, Spanish, French, or Italian. They insisted they knew where we were going and that they wanted to take us. Very much aware of situations like this from the media, I got a little worried. Where will they take us? Should we follow them? Are we going to get robbed? We took the risk. Even then, my priest friend and I already had talked about the tip we were going to give them, as we were sure this is what they came for.

With all of these preconceived ideas, we followed them through more narrow alleys. Surprisingly enough for us, they took us into the church we were seeking. My suspicions disappeared. We were not being robbed, for as I began to look for the kids' tip (a must in most societies when someone tries to help you out), I realized that they had disappeared. Come on, where are they? They did it for the tip; I have it here! Not so. We found them later in the front pew of the church, blessing themselves as Mass began while the assembly joined in singing the penitential rite. How biased I was! Children evangelizing us, adults! I had looked at them as foreigners not to be trusted. Obviously they had learned, even as children, to look into our hearts and perceive what we needed the most.

The scene I just described took place twenty years ago, and it is a lesson I have never forgotten. I want to think that God has helped me grow in my understanding of people. While he still laughs at me when I carry on with my pontifical or liturgical bloopers, I know that he nods at me with a better smile when I try to pierce the outer layers by which my first impressions of people are shaped. I've grown to believe that we are all one on the same journey of faith, hope, and love.

Would it not be awesome if all of us could grow to look at others in this renewed way as we strive to build the kingdom of Jesus in our midst? There is still time; let's give it a try!

---

[1] US Bishops' Committee on Justice and Peace. "Beyond the Melting Pot: Cultural Pluralism in the United States." *Origins*, vol. 10, no. 31 (January 15, 1981).

[2] It would be important to review *The Fourth Instruction for the Right Implementation of the Constitution on the Sacred Liturgy of the Second Vatican Council, Varietates Legitimae, Inculturation and the Roman Liturgy*, by the Congregation for Divine Worship and the Discipline of the Sacraments, published on March 24, 1994. Additionally, among others, consult Aylward Shorter's reflections, *Toward a Theology of Inculturation* (New York: Geoffrey Chapman, 1988) and *Evangelization and Culture* (New York: Geoffrey Chapman, 1994).

WEAVING A TAPESTRY OF INCLUSION IN THE LITURGY

What does it mean to pray as a multicultural assembly?

*I have borrowed the title and most of the contents for this reflection from my presenta-
tion at a symposium held by the Archdiocese of Seattle in July 2004. My comments
constitute a summary of previous reflections shared at a variety of gatherings.
Among them:*

- *The Johannes Hoffinger Catechetical Conference, New Orleans,
  January 9, 2000, "Multicultural and Multilingual: Preparing for
  Worship in the Third Millennium"*

- *The Southwest Liturgical Conference Study Week, Houston,
  January 20–23, 2000, "One Body, Many Faces: Unity in Diversity"*

- *The Deacon/Wives Annual Conference of Region XIII, Salt Lake City,
  July 11–13, 2003*

The daily ferry takes you from Battery Park along the island of Manhattan and makes two important stops. The first stop is the Statue of Liberty, that most impressive monument that stands for everything and everyone for which this country was established, particularly freedom and equality for all. The second stop is Ellis Island, the port of entry from the late nineteenth century until 1954, when it was closed. It served as the portal for thousands of immigrants from Europe, Asia Minor, and other regions of the world.

As you arrive at the island facility, now turned into a museum, you enter two large double doors that lead you to the first of three floors filled with photographs, written stories, drawings and artifacts, all memorabilia from those years and from so many travelers. Your first stop inside the museum is a major section filled with all types of luggage, original pieces brought by the immigrants. Each piece is unique and has the folk art of its country of origin; each represents a different person, a different family, a different name from the one used here in North America. These are names that were quickly transformed by inefficient typists, scribes, and by the growing and complex reality of the world into which they were entering. As you look at this enormous conglomerate of trunks, valises, wooden boxes, and other pieces of luggage, you begin to catch a glimpse of a definite transformation that took place here, an interior process of change that these pieces of luggage seem to hide. For the luggage of Ellis Island—as you and I look back in retrospect—became weighty, not only for the immigrants, but for their descendants. In many cases, these descendants continue to carry it today without understanding fully the why or the how of such immigration. Luggage turned into baggage.

Seeing the baggage of the immigrants recorded at Ellis Island, one must recall the many other Ellis Islands that prevail in our country today—California, Florida, Chicago, Oregon, and the many bodies of water that seem to connect us with them—the Rio Grande, the Gulf of Mexico, the Caribbean Sea, and the Pacific Ocean. We are connected to that conglomerate of "baggage" to which the Church is mandated to preach the Gospel of Jesus Christ, announce the Good News of the kingdom, and invite all who hear the preaching to celebrate the Paschal Mystery in ways in which all can feel at home. What a task for us, pastoral agents of Christ's kingdom, who labor with his love at the beginning of this third millennium! What a mission!

While statistics seem to overwhelm our perception, they might be appropriate at this time. The following numbers were prepared in 2000, and they reflect research that ended in 1998:

- The Hispanic population increased from 22.4 million in 1990 to 30.3 million in 1998, a gain of 35.2 %, or 9 million people

- The Asian and Pacific Islander populations increased from 7.5 million in 1990 to 10.5 million in 1998, a gain of 40.8 %, or 3 million people

- The African American population increased from 30.5 million in 1990 to 34.4 million in 1998, a gain of 12.8 %, or 3.9 million

It is important to note that many, if not most, of the people are Catholic, at least in name.[1]

For this reason, before we touch upon inclusion in the liturgy, we must consider the tapestry that we pastoral agents are called to weave outside the liturgy. Your three key concepts for this reflection, weaving, tapestry, and inclusion at worship, may be translated as being Church and celebrating faith in a multicultural society. The ecclesiological component requires a pastoral commitment (we have to work at being Church); the liturgical component requires us to be as inclusive as Jesus was and as the early Christian community was, particularly at the Eucharist. The concrete, historical, multicultural setting in which we live, affects both components to a degree. Our ecclesial experience occurs within a specific, diverse setting, although our calling to holiness is not determined by that setting. Jesus calls us to become more than what we are, and he assists us in our transition. We begin our conversion journey in a specific social milieu in which he calls us to become holy.

I would like to share a few principles out of which our own reflections emerge. Multicultural worship requires us to be first a multicultural Church. No external arrangement of liturgical elements will help us celebrate our faith in a multi-cultural setting unless we have first addressed the authentic integration of our communities. The ecclesial dimension presupposes our cultural interaction. Just as being a liturgical family presupposes that we are first a family, celebrating faith in a multicultural setting presupposes that we care for and respect one another in a pluralistic setting that displays unity, despite its diversity. The tensions that arise in multicultural worship usually have nothing to do with worship, but they arise from unresolved issues common to multicultural settings.

First we need to address a basic question about our tapestry before we proceed to weaving and our inclusion in the liturgy.

THE TAPESTRY: WHAT IS MULTICULTURAL?

While I enjoy reading letters, I am not the best person when it comes to writing responses. Recently, I have been learning how to use e-mail and have kept up with my correspondence in that manner. As do many of you, I receive innumerable marketing advertisements via the Internet. I also receive many jokes that make me smile at those times I do not feel like smiling (and for which I am grateful), and a few messages that catch my attention. One of these was a sequence of brief letters that children had written to God. As we begin to unveil the subject matter of our gathering—what does it mean to be multicultural in our society and in our Church?—some of these children's brief letters to God might be appropriate:

- "Dear God: Thank you for my baby brother, but what I prayed for was a puppy"   —Nancy

- "Dear God: I bet it is very hard for you to love all the people in the world. There are only four people in our family and I can never do it"   —Bobby

- "Dear God: Maybe Cain and Abel wouldn't kill each other so much if they had their own rooms. It works with me and my brother"   —Eddie

Indeed, children can say things simply and innocently, but they can be profound and challenging, as well. To understand the adjective "multicultural," one must face the issues of "loving all people as God loves us" and "healing the struggles within ourselves and in others" that Cain and Abel so vividly illustrate in the Book of Genesis. Both statements may sound beautiful and romantic, but they are not easy to experience and live out unless the reality has been fostered at home from birth or is the result of an adult conversion. In many cases, what is fostered at home is a series of cultural and emotional family taboos that amount to prejudices. Prejudices are not limited to one or two cultural groups. They appear across the board as they reflect the dark side of people's hearts when they have given in to the sin of racism. An adult conversion, however, as the one Saul of Tarsus experienced on his way to Damascus (see Acts 9), may transform these family taboos into gifts. This transformation requires time and nurturing.

It is important to distinguish two important terms that will help us in our quest. They are "inculturation" and "transculturation." Each of these major words leads us to consider ancillary matters of integration, ethnocentrism, and pluralism. These concepts provide the basis necessary to consider and understand the role of the Catholic Church in contemporary society and the role that each of us plays within the Church and within society.

1. Inculturation is the way in which I have embraced or assimilated my own culture. It may be primary or secondary. Primary inculturation results from the learned behaviors of our cultural patterns. This is the stage at which family taboos are avoided or developed. Psychologists tell us that our early years are formative,[2] to such a degree that the unconscious absorbs everything that we hear or learn from our parents, even if we cannot rationalize it. Secondary inculturation, moreover, results from our willing desire to embrace and attempt to understand the cultural patterns of another person or group in their own milieu or environment. I admire those who embrace secondary inculturation (e.g., missionaries, Peace Corps volunteers), for they are firm enough in their own cultural heritage to help others in theirs.

   What does inculturation entail? I always rely on an article by Jesuit Father Theodore Zuern to explain this process. He envisions every cultural group as being a composite of three layers: the circumference of tangibles, the circle of institutions, and the center of intangibles.

   Imagine, if you please, three concentric circles. At the center of the core is the smallest circle where "the basic beliefs and ideals of a culture, its natural theology, philosophy of life, and the answer to fundamental questions lie." For Father Zuern, while these values are never seen (they are intangible), they are more than frequently misunderstood by many and, yet, they become "the deep motivating force within members of a culture." Around this center appears the circle of structures, the social arrangements made by a culture to display its politics, worship, economics, family style, education, and other institutions. These structures "rise from the intangible values of its culture" and are influenced by several things (e.g., geography, history, climate, etc.). According to

Father Zuern, an outside observer may notice there exists a relation-ship between the intangible values of a cultural group and its social institutions' structure, but this insight is not true in every instance. He observes, "Thus, behavior of one society's members will be unaccept-able to different society's members." When cultures interact with one another, this lack of vision brings about much conflict, for one group may strongly misunderstand the other. He adds, "When distinctive structures are understood by the members of a society, there is no diffi-culty in appreciating why a member acts in a particular, traditional, way... [A]n outside observer who does not understand the expecta-tions, approaches, assumptions, and attitudes involved in this particular mode of action according to the social institutions of this particular cultural society can often wonder or condemn the mode of action."[3]

Finally, around this second circle is the outer circle known as the circle of tangibles, the visible elements of a culture. In Father Zuern's words, "the behavior patterns, the customs, the social habits, fashions, styles, mannerisms, rituals, rites, practices, and conventional usages of materials exhibited by members of a culture." Many tend to compare cultures on the basis of what is tangible and visible to the senses. The heart of the culture, however, does not lie in the ongoing display of its tangible elements, but rather in the roots of its intangibles. And Father Zuern continues, "For all cultures in the Center of Intangibles is a belief about God. A theology becomes an essential part of the culture."[4]

Under the stress of rapid social changes, all of us who should be nurturing one another from the center of intangibles tend to ignore such nurturing to attend to basic needs that are impor-tant to family life. The problem surfaces: while we are attending to such basic needs, we tend to ignore the intangibles that become the basis of who we are as individuals and as a group; thus, the preoccupation for economic enhancement in our homes may lead us to substitute God for other gods that deviate us from his path.

By the same token, we are always challenged to come to know one another beyond the tangibles that confront us and sometimes shock us. So many clergy and laity still relate at the tangible level and refuse to move through the circle of structures to come to know the heart of the other by beginning to appreciate the other's intangibles, even if we cannot agree with them. I propose to you that Jesus did it and sets the example for his disciples and for us.

2. Transculturation[5] is the way in which many cultural groups live together within the same setting, mostly our large cities. This is primarily an urban phenomenon as rural communities may be more resistant to the inclusion of other groups.

   In 1979, the US Bishops' Committee on Social Justice presented an analysis of the options that prevail in our first world society when facing the diversity of cultural groups in our midst; in essence, these options appear frequently in many of our parish communities. Backed by the renewed spirit of the Council and by the contents, among others, of *Gaudium et Spes* (*Pastoral Constitution on the Church in the Modern World*, 1965) and *Evangelii Nuntiandi* (*On Evangelization in the Modern World*, 1975), the bishops of the United States urged all Catholic institutions to recognize these differences and to begin to cope with the multicultural reality of the nation, a reality already in tension at the pastoral level.

   The three options that the bishops provide us in "Beyond the Melting Pot: Cultural Pluralism in the United States (USCCB: 1980) are the melting pot theory, the ghetto theory, and the integration theory. The US bishops opted for the third option as the one that all Christians must strive to discover in their hearts and to promote in their ministry.

   The melting pot theory was prevalent at the turn of the twentieth century. Absorbed by many families from Europe in particular, this theory became the "American" theory. It may be described as lose your original identity and embrace the "American" way by assimilating in all ways into your new, dominant culture. You and others will pass through a funnel and fuse all who are released from that funnel as "typical" American individuals.

   A most revealing phrase is used by Andrew Greeley in his book about the Irish American experience in Chicago, a title that describes, in a way, the melting pot theory in one question: Why can't they be like us? They all have to be like us.[6]

   The ghetto theory asserts, "We don't want to be like you. We only want to be ourselves." These two extreme positions come from a perception of reality that is always right, while everyone else is less right or wrong (epistemological position). The way I perceive reality is the only way that is; everyone else must be incorrect. In anthropology, this posture is known as ethnocentrism.

3. The third option, and the one our bishops proposed in the 1979 document, requires people to consider other perceptions of reality as equal

and as good as their own, although they may not agree with that perception. This alternate posture is known as pluralism, for it allows the opinions of others and permits different groups of people to interact and to learn from one another as they evolve in a transculturating experience. The third option, a result of this posture or attitude, is integration. Integration reflects that we can be ourselves and relate with others and live in peace. We can learn from one another and even modify some of our behavior, but we cannot change from within, from the level of intangibles, for to engage in the process of integration, we need to know and to be proud of our own identity.

Integration points to that process by which people of diverse cultural origins can live together without losing their identity, their way of perceiving and interpreting reality. Some of the images used to describe this process include the salad bowl image and the mosaic image, each valid in its usage. Individually, we are part of a beautiful mosaic that, in its totality, provides wholeness and integrity to the society in which we live.

For a healthy dose of integration, most groups need to respect three criteria: (1) diversity is a gift and not a threat, (2) selectivity must be respected, and (3) some form of liminality must be experienced and expressed.

In essence, a pluralistic community develops openness to diversity as an enrichment of the community and not as a threat. Newcomers provide an opportunity to express the term "catholic" and to echo the unity that comes from professing one faith, sharing one baptism, and believing in the one Lord of all. People who come from different backgrounds to join our parish families should not be seen as a threat to those who welcome them. It would be worthwhile for all of us to promote this principle and to explore it from various angles before we embark on expressing it in worship. While diversity is enriching, no one should compromise its intangibles for the sake of interacting with others; thus, selectivity becomes a necessary ingredient in the process of transculturation. While we respect the thoughts, perceptions, and interpretations of others—and while we may learn from them in the process—we can select out those elements that contradict or become an obstacle to our own identity. We do not have to agree with everything about them. However, this disagreement should not lead to rejection.

Finally, the third criterion is unique to our Catholic experience. Using the terminology provided by the vast literature of Victor

Turner in symbolic anthropology, I shall call "liminality"[7] that in-between phase, that threshold experience, that allows us to separate ourselves from the rhythmical structures of our society so that we may experience our own cultural and religious roots before returning to the everyday rhythmical journey of life.

The word "limen" means "threshold." It was used by Victor Turner to describe the life stages of tribal groups in a chronological pattern of life experiences: birth, puberty, maturity, and death. At each stage, the elders of the group would separate those members of the group who were moving through a given stage to remind them of their heritage—their identity as members of the tribe—and to provide them with symbols that would help them recall and be engaged with that heritage. In this way, they would help prepare them to enter into that new stage with ease, emotional comfort, and security as they would celebrate such passing in what is known as a rite of passage.

During this liminal phase of the rite of passage, individuals are disrobed of all structures; whoever they are or wherever they come from in the hierarchical structure of the tribe becomes insignificant at this phase. At the liminal phase, they are all the same, a homogenous group in search of the intangibles of their own cultural life and, for a while, establishing a *communitas*, a non-structured reality. The elders function as fathers and mothers, as therapists and supervisors, as guides and angels. The result has become evident through many studies: a minimal incidence of dysfunction among tribal groups and no sign of tribal disintegration.

Victor Turner applied this tribal concept to our contemporary society and proposed the following: As we identify our modern life crises that surface at many stages of our human experience, we need to help others pull away from the ordinary structures of society so that they can experience wholeness and peace by getting in touch with the myths and symbols that shape their individuality and their heritage. Liminal experiences, then, become opportunities for them and for us to recharge emotional, cultural, and spiritual batteries so that we can function in society at large without insecurities and discomfort.

Experts have indicated that the four basic life crises of the tribes have been multiplied in contemporary society: birth and childhood, puberty and adolescence, young adulthood, maturity and family life, retirement (and early retirement), aging and, ultimately, death. How do we, pastoral agents of the Catholic Church, as the elders of our own society, help our faithful cope with these multiple life experiences in a faith-filled context? How do we cope with our own life crises and how do we recharge our batteries and the batteries of those we serve at these multiple stages?

I propose that for a healthy integration of our communities and our parishes we need to provide pseudo-liminal moments that can help them move from the stressful settings in which they normally operate to places where they can experience the depth of their identity. I also propose that our Catholic Church already has, in its tradition, such liminal or pseudo-liminal (threshold) moments. However, as pastoral agents, we do not seem to appreciate those moments or take advantage of them in ministry. They should, indeed, shape our own spiritual journey and assist in helping others make that journey throughout their own life experiences: retreats, conversion movements, pilgrimages, and celebrations of patronal feasts. Many of these opportunities are embraced by what is known as popular piety. Even our own liturgical celebrations, Sunday worship, the celebration of the sacraments, the celebrations of the word at funerals, and Life Teen events, are meant to place the faithful in touch with God's life and grace, but also to provide us with the space and time to encounter the Lord and to be transformed by the power of the Spirit.

We ask ourselves, What does it mean to be multicultural? What is this tapestry all about? Do I really believe that, though many, we are one and do I truly know the many who are called to be one? Diversity, selectivity, and liminality, as cultural criteria, do not only constitute key elements for cultural integration, but also provide ways of exploring and fostering cultural integration in our parish communities, parish groups, and ministries as all of us attempt to shape a multicultural vision in the mission of the Church in the United States.

These three criteria stand at the cultural core in our relationship to others in society because they become part of the sets of values that provide self-identity to the core. The first two criteria provide a healthy balance in our growth and acceptance of one another as diverse groups called to become one in faith and action in our diversity. The third criterion addresses not only our meaning in communal celebrations or gatherings, but may also point to a certain ritual behavior that can assist us in our efforts to bring different people together; hence, the well known multicultural worship.

Now that we have explored the tapestry and the elements of multicultural living, let us attempt to explore our calling as Church.

WHO DOES THE WEAVING? WE, THE CHURCH!

The answer to this question engages us into an interior reflection that invites us to determine whether we are going to remain tourists on the circumference of tangibles, in the mission entrusted to us by the Lord, or whether we will work on becoming missionary pilgrims, attempting to reach the center of intangibles of the Church as his disciples did.

Whereas the physical data about humanity through the centuries bears witness to this inclination of the human toward the sacred, we are so blessed to share God's revelation in Jesus Christ. The holy of the First Testament, our revealed God, spoke to us no longer with signs for us to decipher, neither through the whisper of the wind nor through fire, but through his own Son. Jesus, then, makes us aware of his Father and puts us in touch with him through the gift of the Holy Spirit. He calls us through the gift of faith, and we are to respond to him in our service to others. He showed us that we must first accept the cross before we experience resurrection. He sent his apostles to build the Church with Peter as the rock upon which this community would stand firm for all generations to witness. And he remained with us as word and sacrament to be the channel of grace and salvation for all who seek true happiness and true life. As we explore the encounters of Jesus with different persons in the New Testament, particularly in the Gospel of Luke, we discover a series of dialogues with individuals who are foreign to Jewish tradition that help us visualize his call to community from a more universal context.

From his early appearances after the temptation story, Jesus seems to fulfill the law while inviting his disciples to go beyond the law, as they perceived it then. He cures the sick and approaches the many who are rejected by society because they were considered unclean (such as lepers). He invites his followers to love the enemy, to be compassionate, and never to judge; he urges them to produce good fruit, as the trees that surrounded where he preached. He cures the centurion's servant and the widow's son. He welcomes sinners at his table and, while sitting at dinner at a renowned Pharisee's home, he welcomes a woman known to be a public sinner and teaches all those present the great lesson of forgiveness.

In Luke's Gospel, Christ enters a Samaritan town and reprimands his disciples for seeking revenge by calling upon God to exterminate all of its inhabitants. In John's Gospel, he encounters a Samaritan woman and enters into a dialogue with her that changes her life completely. Jesus is close to his friends, Martha, Mary, and Lazarus, as well as to those who seek him out. It matters not if they are alien to his culture and his heritage, such as the Canaanite woman, the man with the shriveled hand, or the man born blind. For Jesus there are no favorites.

His calling is universal, thus, inclusive of all races and cultures; hence, in a way, it is multicultural.

The lessons told in the Acts of the Apostles reiterate the themes of Jesus. Attributed also to Luke, chapter two presents us with the most universal and, thus, multicultural gift that we can receive from Jesus, the gift of the Spirit at Pentecost! We know that the scene is set in contrast to the Tower of Babel in Genesis, but the setting in Jerusalem, where Jews from many parts of the known world had come to hear the apostles, points to the calling of the Church to speak in as many tongues as are necessary to spread the word. Subsequently, after the witnessing of Peter before the Sanhedrin, the martyrdom of Stephen, and the magnificent conversion of Paul, the Book of Acts presents Peter's experience with Cornelius in Caesarea. Cornelius was a centurion of the Roman cohort Italica, who sought God. And God called Peter to visit, preach, and baptize Cornelius and his entire household. The conclusion to chapter ten is interesting as it describes what transpired after the preaching of Simon Peter to Cornelius and his household:

> The circumcised believers who had accompanied Peter were astounded that the gift of the Holy Spirit should have been poured out on the Gentiles also, for they could hear them speaking in tongues and glorifying God. Then Peter responded, "Can anyone withhold the water for baptizing these people, who have received the Holy Spirit even as we have?" He ordered them to be baptized in the name of Jesus Christ.[8]

The preaching of Paul to the Gentiles, despite the opposition of Jewish converts from Jerusalem, and the encounter of Simon Peter with Cornelius open the way for this early Christian community to face, even in the midst of persecution, their first council. The Council of Jerusalem (cf. 50 AD) confirmed that our Catholic Church, as we know it today, is universal, and that "universal" is the calling of the Church that is born out of a pluralistic attitude that makes multicultural happen. But it hasn't always remained as such.

The tensions present in the Book of Acts have appeared through other historical periods when Church leaders and the faithful tended to be exclusive and not inclusive, the product of the various philosophies that culturally affected their thinking at specific times (e.g., Middle Ages or the Reformation), but the Scriptures remain the treasure that we all need to renew the calling that Christ has made to each of us from the moment of our own baptism. In this calling, there lies a universal dimension that must obviously be expressed in our particular lifestyles.

In this context of Jesus and the New Testament Church, having glimpsed at culture as a multicultural reality more than a homogeneous experience, let us dare look at Church in the United States from this perspective. What are our gifts and our challenges?

Our modest reflections attempt to increase our awareness of our approach to ecclesiology. One of the great principles in ecclesiology is being in communion. Perhaps this is the principle that can guide us now. For being in communion for the Catholic Church compels us as pastoral agents

1. To recognize our relationship to the universal Church

2. To accept and recognize the diversity that exists within our unity (unity in diversity), and

3. To express our communion as collaboration and not as competition

A polarity might help us clarify some of these concepts. The opposite of living in communion with the larger image of Church, both in the United States and throughout the world, may be termed "congregationalism" or "parochialism." And the opposite of "collaboration" may be "competition."

I realize that this sounds similar to "What came first, the chicken or the egg?" but we are called to live in communion within our own parish families and to develop a spirit of collaboration. Allow me to suggest a few ways:

1. Welcome newcomers. Hospitality is the key (as Jesus did, so we must do). This is a primary gift in stewardship and we all know it

2. Acknowledge the important role of parish festivals, though presenting merely signs from the tangibles of cultural groups present in the parish, they can become a doorway to accepting and respecting the customs of others as well as an avenue for penetrating the other's circles of understanding and perception

3. Celebrate pseudo-liminal religious and cultural experiences that touch the heart of the various groups present in the community (and invite others to attend and join in prayer). These religious celebrations or festivals are not only a remnant of past devotions but a tool for evangelization[9]

4. Form parish leaders in the criteria of integration. If we can get our pastoral agents first to understand and accept the first criterion of "diversity is a gift and not a threat," we may have resolved half the tension present among them

5. Include all groups in the ministries of the parish community

6. Key leaders from each group participate in the parish pastoral council

7. Engage all groups in social action, involving them in the needs of others, especially as those needs prevail within the social setting in which they live (e.g., assisting the homeless, visiting the elderly, preparing formation programs for the youth)

Being Church in a multicultural community is a gift that we can share with the rest of the world. It is true that many places where our immigrant communities come from may not so readily accept the principles that I have laid out here. The human heart tends to stick to its own and not to share. But Jesus and the early Christian community inspire us to motivate others by example, to try out these principles in practice, and to continue to work hard at making them happen. Jesus, who promised not to abandon us will always to guide us on our journey and will enrich our labor abundantly.

We in the United States have a special gift to share with the universal Church. The Lord is calling us to create a Catholic setting where the unity of our faith is expressed in the diversity of those who are called to share it together. Being multicultural may not be easy, but let us remember that we are not alone in our becoming.

Once the tapestry is woven by us, the Church, we can begin to explore multicultural worship and adapt it in the best possible manner and, within the guidelines of our Roman Catholic liturgy, to our own local settings.

WHAT IS WOVEN? MULTICULTURAL CELEBRATIONS[10]

Each of us is called to tell the story of Jesus in a unique and personal way, though conditioned by cultural symbols that tell the story sometimes better than the words we use. If we agree that in the rituals of our Catholic community, in our worship experience, we recognize both the gift of the Father in Jesus Christ and we offer ourselves with Jesus to the Father to be sanctified by his loving Spirit, then I invite you to reflect on some of the ingredients that are important to consider in the multicultural worship of our pastoral, cultural mosaic:

1. Multicultural celebrations may surface in three different settings:

   • The Pontifical, diocesan, or stational[11] event at which the entire (arch)diocese is invited to participate. Planning these events may become easier because the themes carry the celebration itself rather than the participants who, in most cases, do not know one another very well when they come from distant areas

   • The steady, weekly diet of bilingual Masses that may be more common in areas of the Southwest or the mountain states

- The gathering of the whole parish at key moments of the liturgical year that call for the unity of the community in its diversity, such as at Christmas Midnight Mass, Holy Thursday, the Easter Vigil, the solemnities of Pentecost and/or Most Holy Body and Blood of Christ, or the anniversary of the dedication of the parish or the special celebration of its feast day. As a pastor from the Southeast, these are the celebrations that I have had to plan carefully since they can touch the core of the cultural groups that assemble as one to worship in faith[12]

Some of the elements involved in these preparations require:

- The need for a liturgical committee in which all cultural groups that constitute the community are represented

- The need to study the liturgical season or feast that is being prepared and that calls for multicultural worship

- The need to assess what languages to use, what symbols are inclusive to all, what liturgical aids to prepare, who will be the ministers, how the community is to be prepared for this celebration and what follow up will be given to it that may serve to unify the community in the midst of its diversity.

The answers to these questions require time and preparation

2. The theological principles of the incarnation and the Paschal Mystery of Christ sustain, support, and give credibility to these celebrations. As we die and rise with Jesus, we learn to let go of everything that prevents us from recognizing him in others, particularly our own hang-ups and prejudices. As we celebrate his mystery of unconditional love in the Eucharist, we become aware that his surrendering on the cross brings life to all who share in the same mystery together

3. The *Constitution of the Sacred Liturgy* (*Sacrosanctum Concilium*, 1963) and subsequent documents offer us more principles that can assist us in understanding our need to explore this multicultural reality in the Church: from the key principle of participation (*SC* 14) to the use of the vernacular, to the clarity and simplicity of the rites, to the roles of each minister, and obviously to the need for cultural adaptation (*SC* 37–40), a topic that has become the subject of much discussion as a prelude to the popular topic of inculturation

4. Pope Paul VI's *Evangelii Nuntiandi* and subsequent documents and instruction by Pope John Paul II invite us to consider our need, as

Church, to dialogue with other religions and other cultures in an effort to share the Good News of Jesus with them. Sometimes this ongoing dialogue must be expressed at prayer, especially through the sharing of the word that illumines our daily existence[13]

5. Good multicultural celebrations must be preceded by the growing acceptance of the persons who gather to worship. Much is required of parish leadership, like pastors, school principals, directors of religious education, heads of parish commissions, and parish council members, to make sure the community is working together toward this mutual acceptance, either by collaborating on common projects of social concern or by celebrating God's life in their midst at parish festivals. The externals of such gatherings (i.e., tangibles) truly require an interior conversion of the heart (i.e., intangible) that can be displayed when significant choices that affect all involved are made for the sake of inclusion

6. Multicultural celebrations require the negotiations of all participants. There are no perfect celebrations even if the liturgical commission or team has worked diligently on the structure of the rituals to include everyone present.

   • The Liturgy of the Word may be divided into several languages, although a specific worship aid is needed to make sure all participants understand the proclamation of the readings when done in a language foreign to them

   • The most dominant language, the one that all seem to know the most, should predominate, depending on the circumstances, throughout the entire eucharistic prayer

   • Other languages can be expressed, as usual, in the third form of the penitential rite and in the prayer of the faithful. A common psalm refrain may be balanced by the use of different languages in the verses of the responsorial psalm

   • Other expressions, gestures, and symbols proper to a given culture can enhance the inclusion of that group into the liturgy

The use of Latin may be appropriate, as one of the languages to be used in a multicultural setting, provided the assembly understands what they are singing. This may be accomplished easily through brief phrases or sentences that all can sing.

Like people do in a good marriage, all involved in the preparation of these celebrations must accept and agree upon these negotiations, precisely because the main focus of the celebration needs to express the unity of all in the one Lord. Liturgical preparers should become aware that more is gained than lost at these times. I call it a healthy marriage among members of different cultures within the same community, members that trust one another because they already accept and love one another in the Lord.

CONCLUSION

Luggage is carried by tourists who visit relatives or friends for a while but who cannot relate very deeply to those with whom they visit. In the words of Father Zuern, they are merely confronted by the tangibles of those around them (i.e., the externals, such as food, costumes, music, jokes, and popular refrains) or, if they spend some more time—such as exchange students or Peace Corps volunteers do—they become observers of the structures that constitute the group with whom they visit. Even so, the time spent together is still short and limited.

At the many Ellis Islands of our country, immigrants arrived neither as tourists nor as observers; their encounter was not going to be with the tangibles of a rapidly changing society or with the growing complexity of its social structures. They did not come to visit with relatives and/or friends alone. They came to stay, to start again, to grow and mature into a new reality and, thus, brought with them luggage that turned into baggage, packed from the heart and not from the humble drawers of their original home. The baggage of the heart contains intangible ingredients that cannot be measured by social standards but by other hearts willing to touch upon those elements that bring meaning to the individuals and help them identify the roots of their heritage and traditions; all of the baggage from the heart, the good and the not so good, all to be shared by these immigrants over the many decades of the twentieth century, hoping to become part of a mosaic of living hearts with a living faith!

For this, and for many other reasons, rather than tourists or even immigrants, minorities or refugees, as most people name them, I prefer to call them pilgrims. These are contemporary pilgrims who draw strength from their past to live in the present and who long to build a new future through the religious symbolic language and rituals that shaped their stories at the beginning and now help them overcome crisis moments of anguish and anxiety. We, the Church, must invite them to walk in our own pilgrimage of faith and hope to be enriched by their presence that accentuates our call to be Catholic in our own land.

---

[1] These statistics were released on September 15, 1999 by the United States Department of Commerce News from Washington, DC. The figures may actually have increased since then.

[2] Zuern, SJ, Theodore F., "The Preservation of Native Identity in the Process of Inculturation, as Experienced in American Indian Cultures," *Inculturation: On Being Church in a Modern Society* (Rome: 1983).

[3] Ibid., p. 5.

[4] Ibid., p. 6.

[5] The term is also known as "acculturation" as Melville Herskovits explains while acknowledging the use of this term by the Cuban anthropologist and writer Fernando Ortiz. See: Herskovits, Melville J., *Man and his Works* (New York: Alfred J. Knopf, 1967), p. 529.

[6] Greeley, Andrew M., *Why Can't They Be like Us?* (New York: E.P. Dutton and Company, 1971).

[7] These comments by no means attempt to exhaust the vast literature that Turner provided on this subject. See, among others, Turner, Victor, *The Ritual Process* (New York: Cornell University Press, 1969); *Dramas, Fields and Metaphors* (1974); and Turner, Victor and Edith Turner, *Image and Pilgrimage in Christian Culture* (New York: Columbia University Press, 1978).

[8] Acts10:45–48a of *The New American Bible.*

[9] Pope Paul VI, Exhortation on Evangelization in the Contemporary World (1974), p. 48.

[10] Much has been written about this topic that had its reflective origins in the combined efforts of the Federation of Diocesan Liturgical Commissions (FDLC) and the Instituto Nacional Hispano de Liturgia. See: Francis, Mark, CSV, *Multicultural Celebrations: A Guide* (Washington, DC: Federation of Diocesan Liturgical Commissions, 1998, revised 2000).

[11] The term was restored for usage in the *Ceremonial of Bishops*, although the most common name is "pontifical."

[12] Some reflections about the methodology surrounding these celebrations were published in two articles listed as follows: Sosa, Juan, "Liturgy in Two Languages...Some Principles," *Pastoral Music* (Washington, DC: National Association of Pastoral Musicians [NPM]), August–September 1981, vol. 5, no. 6, and "Liturgy in Three Languages," *Pastoral Music* (NPM), February–March 1983, vol. 7, no. 3.

[13] Although these reflections were written before Benedict XVI became the Roman Pontiff in 2005, one must note that the he has continued this marvelous effort at dialoguing, especially with the Orthodox, Jewish, and Muslim communities.

HISPANIC LITURGY AND POPULAR RELIGIOSITY
A Reflection[1] on the popular piety of Hispanic Catholics in the US

The following reflections were delivered at the 1997 conference on The Hispanic Presence in the U.S. Catholic Church, sponsored by The Catholic University of America and the Instituto de Liturgia Hispana. They were published as an essay in El Cuerpo de Cristo: The Hispanic Presence in the U.S. Catholic Church. I am grateful to Peter Casarella and Raúl Gómez, SDS, its editors, for documenting their annotated contribution. Academic Renewal Press has granted permission for the reprinting of the essay in this publication.

Imagine, if you please, that you are standing before the magnificent cathedral of the small town of Orvieto, not far from Rome, on the solemnity of Corpus Christi, with thousands of people, some of whom are dressed in Medieval costumes representing the various offices and functions of the township, preparing to embark on their annual procession through the streets.

"The ones who are dressed up," someone says, "are all descendants of the original families of Orvieto." "The cardinal will go up to that balcony after Mass," another spectator claims. Indeed, the loudspeakers are blurting brief announcements to guide inhabitants and visitors alike in some form of an orderly fashion (as orderly as you can expect anywhere in Italy).

"What about Mass, the eucharistic liturgy? It must be concluding. Look, there must be some first Communions, too." The bronze gates to the beautiful cathedral open and behind the elaborate canopy that highlights and protects the presider, who is carrying a sumptuous golden monstrance, follow the few thousand worshipers who attended the sacred liturgy inside the cathedral. Such numbers, however, can never supersede the many thousands of pilgrims who are about to enjoy the other sacred liturgy, the liturgy that takes place every Corpus Christi Day outside of the cathedral doors, the very reason, many claim, why people continue to visit Orvieto every year on this solemnity.

Behold, the canopy passes by us. We can see the Blessed Sacrament on top of the monstrance, in the customary *lunetta*. Yet we notice that the monstrance itself is not round, in the shape of the sun, as the monstrances that Latin American communities developed during the centuries of evangelization[2], but rather square, a square and large frame encased in glass. Inside the glass, as if enshrined for all eternity, one can see a piece of cloth covered with blood stains. It is a relic, indeed, the subject of a mythical story that still awes the listener and inspires the believer.

Most people, we notice, have come to see the relic. Do they forget that the Blessed Sacrament stands above it? Not so, but the relic seems to evoke feelings and reactions of tremendous significance for them at a point in this public liturgy in which bodily movement, music, colorful banners, prayer, and tradition blend in space and time in a unique fashion. The Eucharist itself helps them remember the reason for the relic, and the relic, I hope, brings them to a better awareness of the Eucharist.[3]

It was the year 1263 A.D., during the Pontificate of Urban IV, who found himself in Orvieto together with his attendants. A German priest had embarked on a pilgrimage to Rome to recharge his spiritual batteries, for indeed many doubts pursued him. As he stopped in Bolsena to celebrate the Eucharist at St. Christina's Church, he noticed that at the elevation, the host turned to flesh, and blood began to drip consistently from the sacred host on the corporal set on the altar. At the urging of the Pope, the sacred relic of the stained corporal was brought to Orvieto's cathedral where it has remained over the centuries. Under the impact of these events, Pope Urban IV himself established the feast of Corpus Christi for the universal Church one year later. Some even claim that the phenomenon of Bolsena, now in Orvieto, inspired a young theologian named Thomas Aquinas to write one of his most famous poems, Pange Lingua.

The story, the celebration, the liturgy (official and nonofficial) blend together to form a mosaic of faith, unique yet popular, local yet universal in its intent, festive and yet reflective. Myth and ritual imbue themselves in the collective conscience of a people in touch with the fibers of their human experience and motivating them to search for the sacred at its best.[4] Myth and ritual work together to suspend space and time, allowing the divine to appear before the human at its most vulnerable moment of existence, a moment of crisis for the pope, who was besieged by persecutors, and for the priest, who was besieged by unbelief; this was a moment of crisis, perhaps, for a people in search of the divine at a time of misery and oppression. Myth and ritual arise in human tradition to shape the heritage of a community of faith that seeks to transmit its powerful message of hope, as conceived by the repetitive character of its annual celebration.[5]

All of this, and even more, constitutes the dynamic interplay of ingredients involved in the dual treatment of our topic. For the eucharistic phenomenon of Orvieto and its impact on human culture and Church life has been paralleled by the multiple, festive, Church-rooted celebrations that encompass, at least for Hispanics in Latin America and in the United States, a dual experience of worship: Hispanic liturgy and popular religiosity.

While these phenomena of public worship, held outside or inside a church building and alongside so-called official liturgies, provide a sense of pageantry that may satisfy the curious mind, the reality of these two ingredients in today's pastoral life is far from defined, accepted, or understood by all. To say the least, Hispanic liturgy and popular religiosity appear before our bishops, pastors, theologians, catechists, liturgists, and musicians in many parts of the world and, of course, here in the United States, as an ambiguous reality.[6] I would like to examine such ambiguity in three sections: (1) the ambiguous nature of this combination of liturgy and popular religiosity (what is it?); (2) the ambiguous reasoning behind its appearance in the Church and its persistence in the Hispanic heart (why is it what it is? Why has it persisted over time and continued to rise above the reforms of the Church?); and (3) the ambiguous search for a means to approach this phenomenon today (How do we handle it? How do we deal with it now and tomorrow?). Finally, I will offer some conclusions that I hope will summarize my key points in this reflection.

TENSION 1: THE AMBIGUOUS NATURE OF
HISPANIC LITURGY AND POPULAR RELIGIOSITY

The tension about the nature of these two ingredients for worship, some claim, stems out of the growth of the church itself, particularly after the Edict of Constantine in 313 A.D. when, despite much documentation about the catechumenate, the *mystagogia* for neophytes in certain areas where the Church grew rapidly was not deep enough or substantial enough for their understanding. Some writers claim this lack of catechetical depth actually led some of the neophytes to maintain a series of non-Christian practices to which they had grown accustomed before their initiation.[7]

Others claim that the liturgical families of the East and the West during subsequent centuries did not distinguish between what was official or magisterial and what was popular, for there was a continuous and healthy interplay between the two.[8] At any rate, this pre-Medieval period witnessed both the ever-present tension and ultimate rift between the East and the West, manifested at the Council of Chalcedon in 451 by theological discussions and reaching a definite peak in the eighth century when the Eastern emperor attempted to impose a policy of iconoclasm (the abolition of all religious images). Not only did the Church resist such an attempt, but it opted for an elaborate iconography that would be both aesthetic to the eyes and didactic; those who could not read or write would learn about the mystery of God's revelation and love through mosaics and paintings.

We need not turn so far back in time to remember witnessing this tension particularly after Vatican II, when, in the iconoclastic vein of those early centuries or in this century's attempt at simplification, many pastors interpreted the liturgical reform brought about by *Sacrosanctum Concilium* as a justification to get rid of statues, images, novenas, and other devotions, ignoring the call of paragraph 13 of the document to update and reform, not eliminate, the *pia exercitia*.[9] At the same time, we need not forget that still today we witness in many sanctuaries such an overabundance of cluttered symbols. This fact points not only to a misconceived iconography, but to what most would simply consider poor taste, communicating more a sense of the mediocre than a sense of the sacred.

The Medieval reform of Leo IX and, later on, Gregory VII in the early part of the eleventh century provided the Church with both a sense of freedom from the influence of emperors, princes, and political figures and an autonomy that established it as a spiritual society organized with its own legal, juridical, and governing rights. Many claim this centralization of Church life, expressed in institutional centralization and the concomitant development of the liturgy and the spirituality of Christians by the hierarchy and the monks, gave birth to parallel forms of faith-expressions mediated by the cultures of the people: popular religiosity.[10] As a progressive devotion to the humanity of Christ evolved during this Medieval period—a result in part of many apocryphal stories about the birth of Jesus and his passion—a greater sensibility toward sentiments and feelings in public expressions of popular worship also evolved, while the official liturgy of the Church, a patrimony of monks, hierarchy, and the clergy that was celebrated in Latin and transformed by the beauty of Gregorian chant, rooted itself in a reality apart from the feelings of the people.

What did the evangelizers bring to the Americas after 1492? A sense of the sacred permeating the need to convert all native peoples to the one, true faith, probably motivated by the need to face the upcoming end of a century and the apocalyptic spirituality of the era, but also by a sense of freedom (at least before the Council of Trent in 1547) to adapt the rites and symbols of the Church to the needs of her new members in the New World.[11] As the Risen Christ and his pure, Immaculate Mother were substituted for the sun and the moon and the temples of ancient divinities gave way to the building of churches and basilicas, the testimony of many local American saints began to embody the Gospel for the people in unique ways. And even though the official demands of the Tridentine liturgy eventually reached the shores of the new Catholic communities, the people continued to express their new-found faith in Jesus and his Mother with symbols that emerged out of their own cultural-religious experience: *la Cruz de Mayo, los aguinaldos y pastorelas, las novenas y procesiones, el culto a los santos y a sus reliquias, las imágenes y las velas*.[12] They still do this today.

Liturgy and popular religiosity may be perceived from this brief historical perspective as distant as vinegar and oil, or as near as two sides of the same coin. In the hands of pastoral agents, they are not only tools for evangelization now, as they have always been in the past, but sources of deep spiritual nourishment that place us all in touch with the core of human experience, our religious self. Particularly among Hispanic Catholics, liturgy and popular religiosity are and should be viewed as complementary and not exclusive of one another.

In describing our first tension, and in attempting to answer the question "What is it?" we can say that, among Hispanics, liturgy and popular religiosity embody a language of worship that is unique and enriching, open-ended and thus accessible to growth, a marriage and not a divorce (as in early Medieval times), sisters that, though siblings, are not in competition with one another, unless our pastoral leaders make them compete by ignoring and neglecting them.

In the last few decades, these two components have become the source of theological interest as a result of the reflection of Latin American Church leaders and as a reaction to secularism at all levels of life.[13] However, one must admit that the connection is mentioned only lightly in the Medellín documents of 1968, officially targeted by the magisterium for the first time by Pope Paul VI in 1974 both in *Marialis Cultus* and in *Evangelii Nuntiandi,* explored more fully by the gathering of bishops at Puebla in 1979, most recently assumed under the heading of inculturation by John Paul II, and constantly referred to by liturgists, pastors, and some theologians in their writings.[14] Nonetheless the interplay between liturgy and popular religiosity continues to be ignored by most Church leaders and pastoral agents today even though it is still extremely important for many people. Even for the sects and other syncretistic groups, it has become an avenue of recruitment and integration into a new identity.

TENSION II: THE AMBIGUOUS REASONING BEHIND ITS APPEARANCE IN THE CHURCH AND ITS PERSISTENCE OVER THE CENTURIES (THE WHY AND THE WHAT)

Certain sciences, such as anthropology, sociology, and psychology, among others, can definitely assist theology in its quest to reinterpret the interaction between liturgy and popular religiosity.

Three reasons, among many, seem to prevail as ways of answering the question that permeates our focus now: why? The heart of the answer lies in understanding the religious person (*homo religiosus*)[15] in all of his or her complexity as the religious person faces him or herself and others under these global realities.

THE NEED FOR SALVATION

More than ever, today one feels the hunger for spirituality and meaning in people. Furthermore, Hispanic Catholics find themselves at the crossroads of life when, after leaving their culture of origin, they tend to neglect and abandon the foundations of their "meaning" level, the religiosity that fosters and sustains their identity. They proceed to substitute their religious heart for economic improvements at the risk of losing the best of their heritage and tradition. Some in the past had been forced to abandon externally the expression of that religious heritage under the assimilating pressures of a society foreign to them and hostile to their development. In the present, many Hispanics themselves seem to buy into our consumer-oriented society as the answer to all problems. More evident in the urban centers of our country toward which Hispanics move in ever greater numbers, the result of this process is dismal: the disintegration of their personal and family life, which, in turn, echoes in them the need to find wholeness and harmony by rediscovering their myths and rituals in a new way and under new circumstances. Who can help? If we, the Church, are not present to them, someone else will be.

INCLINATION TOWARD THE SACRED

The sacred is not institutional nor can it be institutionalized. People have their own inspiration and treasure of faith-expressions. In the sacred, the religious person experiences a proximity to nature, lost in most of our industrial society at large. Before the sacred, the religious person becomes a protagonist at worship, not a spectator. The religious person, especially, though not exclusively, under a crisis, seeks to receive the unveiling of the mystery as the healer of all crises. In the sacred, those categories of social life by which we distinguish one another, such as race, denomination, social and economic status, disappear, for all religious persons experience the oneness of God. As tribal members set aside time and space to experience "liminal" moments by which they could be in touch with the power of their roots, transmitted by their elders,[16] Hispanic Catholics today seek to withdraw from the deafening noises of human life to experience the "rumor of angels," the whisper of God and the affirmation of their present reality. They recognize in the sacred that ultimate reality without which they could not live and toward which they journey. In the sacred, they begin to find themselves, if their elders are willing to lead them to the sacred.

WORSHIP/RITUAL AS LIBERATON AND TRANSFORMATION

As rational, logical, disciplined, and orderly existence becomes unbearable, the source of constant strain and continuous pain for Hispanic Catholics at the non-rational level (e.g., sentiments, feelings, passions) and the search for liberation and peace from this personal and family crisis begins. When confronted with the difficulty of human existence and without much solution, Hispanic Catholics find in religious rituals both the gift of God as presence and the space and time to play in the midst of strains and tensions. Religious rituals liberate them and allow them to mediate through their own culture their perception of God and humanity. Religious rituals allow them to speak a language distinct from that of society, not the language of economics or technology but a language of faith, which remains understood only by those who share the same faith. It also allows them to mediate, through their own culture, those symbols that emerge out of their own collective memory and identify them as one.

In answer to our second question, the why of the what, we must turn not only to history but rather to the signs of the times. In times of crisis, our people seek more than an answer, a way toward liberation. They bring to our table their own dialogue with human existence and religious symbols. Are we prepared to dialogue with them?

The U.S. Church, through our Hispanic Catholics, is witnessing an ongoing tension that requires attention and focus. In the dialogue between liturgy and popular religiosity, we need to perceive other ongoing dialogues that should become part of the pastoral life of the Church in a more serious way. We need to address the broader dialogue between faith and culture that calls for a reinterpretation of our pastoral life in light of the needs of the people and not of our needs, as structured by previous experiences not present today. Secondly, we also need to enter into the dialogue between our Catholic culture and non-Christian cultures still prevalent in the religious symbolism of our Hispanic Catholics, who, in turn, come from areas of Latin America in which several cultures and non-Christian religious practices prevail, some of native American ancestry, others of African roots.

I propose that we are still in diapers about this last dialogue, and the previous one has merely begun to catch our attention. I would furthermore like to propose that popular religiosity and liturgy, rather than remaining opposed and distant elements of our pastoral life, can become for us the avenue through which we can reinterpret those stories and symbols that shape the Hispanic worldview. I venture to propose that, for Hispanic Catholics, this constitutes the avenue to a healthy inculturation of the Gospel and the path to the new evangelization so badly needed in our culture of death.

TENSION II: THE AMBIGUOUS SEARCH FOR A MEANS TO
APPROACH HISPANIC LITURGY AND POPULAR RELIGIOSITY TODAY
(HOW THE WHY AND THE WHAT CAN MAKE SENSE)

The essence of this third section lies in a tension that we have discussed before at previous meetings of the Instituto de Liturgia Hispana, first in Albuquerque, New Mexico, in 1984 and later, in Phoenix, Arizona, in 1992:[18] the balance between tradition and creativity.

"Tradition" does not mean "archaic," "old-fashioned," or "obsolete." Tradition is dynamic and, by its very nature, encompasses the core heritage of a people's belief system.[19] Popular religiosity, more than liturgy, has embodied the best of the Hispanic traditions, particularly during the last five hundred years. The various groups of Hispanics all feel at home at one another's popular celebrations of faith. Tradition may have its limitations: it may not lend itself to innovations, but properly guided by authentic elements of faith and the patience of pastoral agents, it may become open-ended to accept new forms of expression.

"Creativity," on the other side, does not mean "anarchy," "relativism," or "individualism." Creativity is based on a healthy appreciation of diversity as a criterion channeled both by anthropology and theology. Through creative endeavors that respect the best of the tradition and use the core of symbolic expression, Hispanic Catholics can rediscover themselves on a journey of spiritual enrichment.

Consider a concrete example: A Good Friday procession begins at the conclusion of the English Good Friday service. One allows the English-speaking participants to carry the statue of Christ out of the church into the street while the image of Mary, already outside of the church and surrounded mostly by the Hispanic members of the community, awaits. An image of Saint John the Evangelist is carried by the youth of the parish, who long to be near to the Lord and not give up on life despite family and social difficulties and misunderstandings. Here we Hispanics are trying to be creative within a traditional framework of liturgy and popular religiosity. Such is a service that, at the conclusion of this triple-imaged procession, the English-speaking participants go home, the Hispanics enter the church for their liturgical service, and the youth reflect on prayer and fasting in a different setting. But, for once, they have found unity and support around the imagery of their cultural and Catholic tradition.

Tradition and creativity must remain in constant dialogue with each other. We, the Church's pastoral agents, must make it happen; this is a dialogue of deep respect for the many prayerful forms that the people display in their search for a new beginning and a better tomorrow.

The Roman Missal of Paul VI provides us with avenues of adaptation for the interplay between liturgy and popular religiosity to happen at the level of both cathedral and parish celebrations.[20] The openness in the monitions (the carefully crafted texts at certain celebrations in which the Introductory Rites involve the entire assembly in body and song, such as the Blessing of Palm Branches on Palm Sunday, the Blessing of Candles on the Feast of the Presentation of the Lord, the Blessing of the New Fire at the Easter Vigil) provide us with good models of interaction. The *Book of Blessings* and the subsequent revision of other rites, such as the Marriage Rite, will continue to provide us with good spaces in which the people can find their role as a ministerial assembly. But these texts are not enough; more work must continue in bringing the rites of our Church closer to the people for whom they are intended.

In essence, the efforts of the Instituto de Liturgia Hispana and collaborative academic bodies, such as The Catholic University of America, must continue to ensure that the how of the what may find expression once the why is more and more appreciated by our people. The efforts of all pastoral agents in their spiritual growth and the service of God's people must become apparent for many other organizations to focus on the promotion of this interplay between liturgy and popular religiosity as the treasure of an authentic spirituality among our Hispanic Catholics.

CONCLUSIONS

The challenge is ours to face and to confront. Before a culture of death, on the way to the third millennium and called to announce and recreate a civilization of love, are we willing to take Hispanic liturgy and popular religiosity seriously?

Hispanic liturgy and popular religiosity are not only here to stay, but to grow. Just as one cannot abandon liturgy to itself, for it might tend to lack its focus (the people for whom it is intended), one cannot abandon popular religiosity to itself, for it can be easily manipulated by other entities and for other ends that might deviate it from its liberating power.

The anthropological and theological analysis, already available from the Mexican-American perspective and the Caribbean worldview,[21] among others, must reach our seminaries and the curriculum of all universities and centers of learning. Our future priests must understand how our people move and are moved at worship. Our pastoral agents must also learn how not to rationalize liturgy and popular religiosity and, thus, not to relegate them to Cinderella roles, the filler courses and independent studies, thereby diminishing their importance in relation to other areas of theological research.

All of us must heed the voice of the liturgical reform uttered by *Sacrosanctum Concilium* and the subsequent documentation discerned and issued by the post-Conciliar group of *periti* known as the *Consilium*.[22] If the motivating force of the reform became grounded in the criteria of participation, the rediscovery of the Scriptures, the use of the language of the people, the development of ministries, and the cultural adaptation currently referred to as "inculturation," then we would already have with us an overwhelming treasure of spiritual wealth in the interaction between liturgy and popular religiosity.

Lastly, all of us must heed the voice of our people, whom we serve and for whom we exist. In their need, they cry for worship that can heal them and free them. In their joy, they long for worship that can help them share their humanity through its best possible cultural mediation: their symbols. And in their hope they look toward us with pride so that we can help them become pilgrims of love on this journey to the new millennium, not messengers of despair and death. Are we willing and ready to walk with them these extra miles by reaching out to them at the deepest core, their circle of intangibles, and help them experience the liberating presence of the Spirit-at-Work within and among them through the powerful interplay between our/their Hispanic liturgy and our/their popular religiosity?

A Recent Note from the Author:

One must note that since this publication and the many other reflections on popular piety that have surfaced over the last three decades, the Congregation for Divine Worship and the Discipline of the Sacraments released and published Directory on Popular Piety and the Liturgy, Principles and Guidelines *on December 17, 2001. This directory, a must in seminaries and many other programs of formation, is available both in English and Spanish.*

---

[1] The following sources were useful in preparing this article: Jose Manuel Bernal, "Iniciación al Año Litúrgico" (Madrid: Ediciones Cristiandad, 1984); J. Castellano, "Religiosidad Popular y Liturgia," *Diccionario de Liturgia: Documentos completos del Vaticano II* (Bilbao: Ediciones Mensajero, 1980); Richard P. McBrien, Catholicism, rev. ed. (New York: HarperCollins, 1994); A. G. Martimort, *The Church at Prayer*, one-volume ed., ed. A. G. Martimort (Collegeville: Liturgical Press, 1992); Juan J. Sosa, "Liturgia Hispana en Estados Unidos," Notitiae: Sacra Congregatio ProCulto Divino 20 (1984): 688–96; Juan J. Sosa, "Renewal and Inculturation," in *Liturgy: A Journal of the Liturgical Conference 9*, no. 2 (1990): 17–23; P. Manuel Traval y Roset, Milagros Eucarísticos (Quito, Ecuador: Librería Espiritual, 1989).

[2] See Jaime Lara, "The Sacramented Sun: Solar Eucharistic Worship in Colonial Latin America," in *El Cuerpo de Cristo: The Hispanic Presence in the United States Catholic Church* (New York: Continuum, 1998.

[3] For the relationship of popular devotions to the liturgy see *Sacrosanctum Concilium* (SC), in *Documents on the Liturgy* 1963–1979: *Conciliar, Papal, and Curial Texts* (DOL), camp. the International Commission on English in the Liturgy (Collegeville: Liturgical Press, 1982), 1.13.

[4] See Theodor H. Gaster, *Thespis: Ritual, Myth and Drama in the Ancient Near East*, rev. ed. (New York: Harper & Row, 1961); Ronald L. Grimes, *Beginnings in Ritual Studies*, rev. ed. (Columbia, SC: The University of South Carolina Press, 1995).

[5] See Victor W. Turner, *The Ritual Process: Structure and Anti-Structure* (Chicago: Aldine, 1969).

[6] The fourth instruction on the implementation of *Sacrosanctum Concilium* (SC), *Instruction: Inculturation and the Roman Liturgy* (Washington, DC: United States Catholic Conference Office of Publishing and Promotion Services, 1994), §45, appears to modify SC 13 in its approbation of popular devotions that accord with the liturgy. Though neither SC 13 nor the fourth instruction prohibit the practice of employing popular devotions as a source of inculturation of the liturgy, they certainly add to the ambiguity.

[7] See especially Josef A. Jungmann, *The Early Liturgy: To the Time of Gregory the Great*, trans. Francis A. Brunner (Notre Dame: The University of Notre Dame Press, 1959).

[8] See for example Adolf Adam, *Foundations of Liturgy: An Introduction to Its History and Practice,* trans. Matthew J. O'Connell (Collegeville: Liturgical Press, 1992); Anscar J. Chupungco, *Worship: Progress and Tradition* (Washington, DC: Pastoral Press, 1995); and Herman A. J. Wegman, *Christian Worship in East and West: A Study Guide to Liturgical History,* trans. Gordon W. Lathrop (Collegeville: The Liturgical Press, 1990).

[9] DOL 1.13.

[10] See for example Anscar J. Chupungco, *Liturgical Inculturation: Sacramentals, Religiosity, and Catechesis* (Collegeville: Liturgical Press, 1992); A. G. Martimort, "Definitions and Method," in *The Church at Prayer.*

[11] See Jaime Lara, "Precious Green Jade Water: A Sixteenth-Century Adult Catechumenate in the New World," *Worship* 71 (1997), 415–28.

[12] ...the May Cross, the gifts and mystery plays, novenas and processions, the cult of the saints and their relics, images and candles.

[13] For an overview of the importance of popular religion to Hispanic/Latino theological reflection see Arturo J. Banuelas, "U.S. Hispanic Theology: An Initial Assessment," in *Mestizo Christianity: Theology from the Latino Perspective,* ed. Arturo J. Banuelas (Maryknoll, N.Y.: Orbis Books, 1995), 53–82.

[14] For a summary and interpretation of these see Michael S. Driscoll, "Liturgy and Devotions: Back to the Future?" in *The Renewal that Awaits Us,* ed. Eleanor Bernstein and Martin F. Connell (Chicago: Liturgy Training Publications, 1997), 68–90.

[15] This term was coined by Mircea Eliade; for an interpretation of Eliade's concept see David Cave, *Mircea Eliade's Vision for a New Humanism* (New York: Oxford University Press, 1993).

[16] Liminality as a ritual concept was introduced by Arnold Van Gennep and further developed by Victor Turner and Ronald L. Grimes. See Arnold Van Gennep, *The Rites of Passage,* trans. Monika B. Vizedom and Gabrielle L. Caffee (Chicago: University of Chicago Press, 1960); Victor Turner, *The Forest of Symbols: Aspects of Ndembu Ritual* (Ithaca, NY: Cornell University Press, 1967); Ronald L. Grimes, *Beginnings in Ritual Studies.*

[17] This conference, entitled Somos Peregrinos: La Conferencia Nacional de Liturgia Hispana, took place from 27–30 September 1984.

[18] This conference, entitled Quinta Conferencia Nacional: La Religiosidad Popular de los Hispanos: Mitos, Simbolos y Creatividad, took place from 25–28 October 1990.

[19] See Chapungco, *Worship: Progress and Tradition,* as well as Espin, *The Faith of the People,* for particularly germane analyses of tradition and creativity.

[20] Of particular interest is the *General Instruction of the Roman Missal,* ch. 2, DOL 208.7–57.

[21] The work of Virgilio Elizondo, Arturo Perez, and the Instituto de Liturgia Hispana can be useful for seminaries and universities addressing the question of the anthropological and theological aspects of Hispanic devotional practices and liturgy.

[22] *Consilium ad exsequendam Constitutionem de sacra Liturgia* (The Council for the Implementation of the Constitution on the Sacred Liturgy). See Annibale Bugnini, *The Reform of the Liturgy 1948–1975,* trans. Matthew J. O'Connell (Collegeville: Liturgical Press, 1990), 49–53.

EUCHARIST AS GIFT AND CHALLENGE

A reflection on the gift of the Eucharist for all and the pastoral challenge of understanding the Eucharist vis-à-vis the popular piety of our Hispanic Catholics

Most of the following reflections were delivered during the eucharistic congress of the Diocese of Phoenix, Arizona, on May 29, 2000. The section "Eucharist and Popular Piety" was part of the essay prepared for publication in Book of Readings on the Eucharist *(Washington, DC: USCCB Publishing, 2000). In these reflections, I do not pretend to provide a theological treatise on the Eucharist; I simply aim to translate my love for the Eucharist 2 the challenges that anyone's love for the Eucharist may face in today's society.*

It is indeed a privilege for me to be with you for this marvelous eucharistic congress. After visiting a few other communities this year at similar gatherings, I can honestly say that I come to you as a pastor, a teacher, and as someone in love with worship in all of its aspects. I gather with you, mindful of the spiritual well-being of all who seek out true happiness internally, in their human relationships and, above all, with God. I come to the Valley of the Sun from the southeastern coast of Florida. I have come as I believe that we all need to stop the ordinary rhythm of our lives to reflect upon Jesus, the risen Lord who, as Eucharist, is our sustenance and strength. The Eucharist is a gift from God to humanity but a challenge for humanity to embrace, particularly for us as the disciples of Jesus.

We need to communicate and dialogue in a religious language we can all understand. As we dialogue, we can begin to understand what Jesus wanted from each of us, as he remained among us in the Eucharist and sends us forth from the Eucharist to be his living sign in the world. Our communication must be clear, grounded on the Scripture and the dynamic tradition of our Church.

Do we really believe in what we teach and proclaim? How much do we need to share in the whole vision of Eucharist as we grow spiritually? Although Eucharist is a mystery we can never fully resolve, as a mystery, it must be loved and lived.

Eucharist is the mystery of the permanent presence of God's unconditional love in our midst through the sacrifice of his own Son, Jesus Christ. Let us just take that statement for a moment:

- Eucharist as "presence," transformed and transforming, hidden and made evident through the simple signs the Lord himself chose to remain among us

- Eucharist as a "permanent" presence, transcending time and history, allowing us to be part of the Last Supper while commemorating the ongoing crossing of a threshold, the passage with Jesus from slavery to freedom, from sin to grace, from darkness to light

- Eucharist as "the permanent presence of God's unconditional love," for when all the spoken prayers cease and the gestures conclude, when all the music stops, there is still Jesus, permanently present among us to remind us that we are never alone, that he accompanies, animates, challenges, and heals us. He is here forever to remind us of his unconditional love, a love that, as Saint John wrote, was expressed in action as well as in words. We need to reflect on the Eucharist so that, in carrying out the Lord's command ("Do this in memory of me"), we may learn to become that which we actually share; we may learn to become Eucharist to others, selflessly and generously

Many choices we make in today's society are based on our personal convenience and come at the expense of others, as was the case with the apostles before Pentecost. Jesus consistently reminded them of their calling. When the apostles indicated there was nothing left to eat, Jesus urged, "Give them some food yourselves." They could not understand him fully because they were too busy dealing with the problem ahead of them (feeding the multitude) instead of discovering options or possibilities that their trust in the Lord and in themselves could provide to overcome such problem (see Matthew 14).

What Pope John Paul II called the "culture of death" I can easily translate as "the culture of disposables." We dispose of what inconveniences us, and we keep what is most convenient for our business and for our success. We not only dispose of diapers and old clothes, but also of food past its expiration date, in spite of so much hunger throughout the world. We dispose of enormous amounts of paper though it could be used by the poorest countries of the world. We even attempt to dispose of people, like the unborn, who cannot speak for themselves, or the elderly, who some consider have nothing worthwhile to say. Simply watch television a few minutes to absorb the culture of disposables in which we are striving to understand, speak about, and become Eucharist. What a challenge, indeed!

If we look deeply into our own hearts, we will probably discover that we share in this culture more than we really want to. At times, we stand in arrogance before others, flaunting our Christian roots, yet demons crawl inside us, dissuading us from taking action that we proclaim with our lips. I use the word "demons" symbolically, as images of temptation, nonetheless real in our daily lives.

In this culture of disposables, we are seduced and persuaded to follow three significant personal and social demons against the faith we have in the risen Lord and the faith we express and share at the Eucharist. I call these demons the three *E*'s. They are the demons of egotism, ethnocentrism, and exclusivism.

Egotism: A Demon of Self-Centeredness

Egotism may be described as the desire to satisfy oneself so much that the needs of others do not count. The expression "I want" becomes the guiding principle. It is an attitude that children often have because of their young nature, but they usually outgrow it. In adults, it is an attitude of arrogance that sees others as disposable creatures that have nothing to add to life. "I want" people only think of and for themselves. Because of the culture of disposables, "I want" people cannot understand the word or the concept of sacrifice. Even in the New Testament, Saint Paul reminds us that the cross became an absurdity to many and a scandal to others; it remains as such today for those who cannot find in the cross a symbol of victory and sacrifice (see 1 Corinthians 1:18).

Egotism or selfishness led to problems in Corinth when the community experienced division and inequality as they shared the meal of Jesus. Saint Paul confronted them with this problem in his first letter and challenged them to change their ways. They could not share the Eucharist with such animosity (1 Corinthians 11:17–34). Neither can anyone of us, anywhere in the world.

The Eucharist stands against this demon! The Eucharist we share confronts us with the sacrifice of Jesus, who became both the victim and the priest of sacrifice (Hebrews 7:26–27). He embraced all other sacrifices as the lamb taken to be slaughtered out of love for all humanity (Hebrews 9:11–15).

Eucharistic people do not give up on life, especially when it gets hard to live. They do not give up on marriage; they work at it. They do not give up on friendships or family relationships just because there is a disagreement. Eucharistic people do not give up on faith or Church just because there are differences expressed in specific circumstances. Eucharistic people refuse seduction by the demon of egotism and embrace the mystery of Jesus in its totality, never giving up on any experiences or any person that brings hardships to their journey in life.

Ethnocentrism: A Demon of Society

The second demon has affected us for a long time. Ethnocentrism may be described by anthropologists as a belief that one's culture is better than any other culture. Some typical statements that reflect this attitude are "I am better than you," "You have nothing to offer to me," and "I do not want to mingle or live with people who are different from me." This demon is also be seen as racism or prejudice. It can eat at anyone's heart and consume it with hatred while providing distinct justification with expressions like "I have always lived here" and "Why can't they be like me?"

Eucharist must be at the center of our lives and at the heart of our commitment. As we address issues on multicultural and multilingual experiences in our cities—as well as in our parishes—we can honestly raise the question, How can any cultural group share in the Eucharist and stand divided by the demons of ethnocentrism, racism, or even prejudice? Many ask us today, "How can we be one, though we are many, coming from different backgrounds, languages, and colors?" The answer lies in the very nature of the Church: because we are in communion with one another through the Lord Jesus Christ (1 Corinthians 12:27–31).

Let us learn from the master himself. The mandate of Jesus is prayer, "that all may be one as you, Father, are in me, and I in you" (John 17:21). Eucharist brings us together in a bond of unity that can only be broken by our willingness to be separated from the source of love that beckons us to be in communion, despite our differences and our disagreements. As Jesuit Father Zuern said in "The Preservation of Native Identity in the Process of Inculturation," we need to learn to treat one another from the inner level of our cultural experiences instead of just from the outer layer of the tangibles that at times distinguish us externally. We need to discover resurrection power in the intangibles of our own journey so that we can appreciate it in others with whom we are called to build up the body of Christ.[1]

As we come together to communicate and share with others in their journey of life and faith, a definite healing will come out of this process that will bring us to the Eucharist with a different attitude; true reconciliation will follow. Similarly, we must trust that Eucharist will bring about healing as we negotiate our multicultural position. Healing that leads to reconciliation requires both recognition of our own mistakes and sharing of forgiveness. Eucharist calls us to a bond that seems an impossible task to reach, but it is not impossible when the Lord is in our midst and when the Church echoes his prayer of unity to foster a true communion of hearts and minds in the Lord.

EXCLUSIVISM: A DEMON OF EXTREMES

This demon may be termed fundamentalism in all aspects of life, but particularly in the area of religion. As with any other "-ism," this demon places us at the center of life and pushes Jesus to the sidelines. It makes us echo phrases such as, "You are wrong, and I am right." It pushes us to use words like "conservative" and "liberal." It corners us into one of the two sides and forces us to make choices we do not want to make. It places authority in only a vertical mode and excludes who can share in it, particularly women. This demon often appears disguised as traditional or Scripture-based. It is confusing, dangerous, narrow-minded, and limited in scope. It may indeed remind us of the Pharisaic attitude found in the

New Testament, against which Jesus spoke so vehemently, always condemning the attitude but extending his hand in reconciliation to those who displayed it.

Once again, Eucharist stands against this demon of exclusivism by calling us to form a bond of love. Out of love for one another in Jesus, we pass from death to life, from sin to grace, from darkness to light, from prejudice to hospitality, and from excluding others to including them into our mission.

Greek literature provides us with at least three different terms for the word "love."[2] When poets or writers used "eros," they expressed "love of the flesh." When they used "philos," they intended to address the relationship of family members and friends, beyond the flesh, and when they used "agape," they pointed to a love without boundaries, an unconditional love that cared for others more than for oneself. As the Greeks heard the story of Jesus and began to share the Eucharist, they began to understand agape, but also called the Eucharist by the name. Only in agape can we overcome the demon of exclusivism.

Eucharist stands against the demons of egotism, ethnocentrism, and exclusivism, inviting us to become a sacrificial people who grow and relate to strangers. We are to welcome them into our hearts as well as to our table. We are to be an inclusive people willing to take risks to build bonds of love in the midst of our culture of disposables. In doing so, the Eucharist empowers us to overcome the demons so that we may sing the praises of the Lamb who stands victorious in his sacrifice of love.

IN CHRIST'S RESURRECTION WE REJOICE!

Throughout the Easter season, we come to know Jesus as:

- The servant who taught his disciples to wash each other's feet (John 13:2–15)
- The risen master who empowered Mary and the disciples to announce his life to others (John 20:21)
- The Lord who brings peace to his disciples and invites them to share that peace always (John 20:19)
- The Good Shepherd who invites us all to listen to his voice (John 10:11)
- The voice who helps us bear good fruit if we remain in him (John 15:8)
- The Christ who ascends to the Father and prays for us to become one (John 17:11)

.These powerful images have enriched our liturgical celebrations, especially our Sunday Eucharist. It is the mystagogy, the catechetical instruction of the Church that, from earliest times, elicits an act of true faith based not just on words, but on action. Our Church wants us always to remember that Jesus died and rose to teach us how to die and rise with him each day. Have we listened to his voice, as the neophytes, our newly baptized members, have? Do we listen to that voice in the silence of our prayer life, in the pains and joys of our own peers, in the strangers who seek us out to guide them, in the hungry and the thirsty, even in those for whom Eucharist means nothing and, who, by their indifference, help us value how much it means for us?

I hope that today, through the experience of this marvelous eucharistic congress, we can listen to his voice beckoning us to respond in faith and action as he lifts us up to the Father in his sacrificial love. He calls us each by name, calling all of us together as a Church and speaking to us in many ways. Pray with me that we may always be disposed to listen!

EUCHARIST AND POPULAR PIETY[3]

The communion to which we are called as Christians is not based on external symbolism, such as looking alike, talking alike, praying alike, or acting alike. These manifestations can never stand as the ultimate criteria for a healthy Church community. The bonding of all Christians in Christ's agape must arise out of a rediscovery of Christ's presence within the historic traditions of the Church and within the religious traditions of the cultures that have embraced the faith. While each cultural group will have different expressions of faith, depending on the strength of its popular piety, many common elements are shared among cultural groups who profess the Catholic faith and assemble to celebrate the mystery of Christ in their lives.

The multicultural society in the United States undoubtedly presents a challenge to the Church that openly announces the saving presence of Jesus in all languages and to all cultures. Young and old, Hispanics, Native Americans, Haitians, singles, and married couples continue to relate at least to some of the devotions that are passed from generation to generation. It is precisely in this popular piety that the Church finds a tool for evangelization,[4] for it can observe their most significant symbols and transform them to assist in their self-expression. If we were to explore and enrich such expressions with new and creative forms of praise and worship, these cultural groups might find themselves more comfortable at public prayer. In essence, the more they can identify with their religious identity, the more they will be able to experience the unity to which the Gospel of Jesus Christ calls them in their new setting in the United States. Of course, as pastoral agents continue to explore the renewal of popular piety, a subsequent challenge remains: how can the popular piety of a given cultural group relate to the Paschal Mystery that is particularly expressed at the Eucharist, toward which all piety must lead?

Popular piety is said to have emerged in the West after the fifth century. While the liturgy of the Church had borrowed symbols and customs from Jewish, Roman, and Greek traditions at first, it took on a distinctive character at this time. It became separated from the devotions of the laity; its language was foreign to most people, and it was reserved primarily for the hierarchy and the clergy. While Eastern liturgies continued to incorporate elements of popular devotions into their worship, the West decided to do without them. In essence, this attitude gave way to the birth of newer forms of public expression, such as processions and religious dramatizations, that characterized the popular expressions of the people throughout the Middle Ages.

If this division had become apparent from the fifth century on, it became inevitable after the Council of Trent (1545–1563). The faithful at that time were required to fulfill the minimum expression of faith: to be present at the liturgy externally. In fact, the interior disposition of the Christian had found meaning and solace in other devotions that had begun to substitute for the liturgical celebrations, which were not understood. Popular piety took the place of the official liturgy and continued to grow in the Church community as a parallel form of prayer.

In time, the Church has maintained these popular devotions as valid devotions that must, however, culminate in the official prayer of the Church, the prayer *par excellence*, the liturgy. Aware of this historical division, the Church made repeated attempts to reconcile popular piety with liturgical piety, always avoiding to reduce one to the other, or to substitute one for the other. Pius XII, in *Mediator Dei* (1947), and the Council Fathers of Vatican II, echoing Pius X's motu propio of 1903, expressed the need to keep popular piety distinct from liturgical piety, but not in conflict.[5] As we have already seen, the Second Vatican Council attempted to thwart efforts to do without all of these devotions and to reduce them exclusively to the liturgy. In the creative interplay of liturgy (particularly the Eucharist) and those popular seasonal expressions of the faithful may lay a balanced spirituality for many of our Catholic assemblies. The bishops of Latin America, gathered in Puebla de los Angeles, Mexico, in 1979 began to describe this balance as follows:

> …We can point to the following items as positive elements of the people's piety: the Trinitarian presence evident in devotions and iconography; a sense of God the Father's providence; Christ celebrated in the mystery of his Incarnation…in his crucifixion, in the Eucharist

and in the devotion of the Sacred Heart. Love of Mary is shown in many ways...[6]

How, then, are we to answer the question of popular piety's relation to the Paschal Mystery? Allow me to attempt to answer it as follows, in the midst of all of the challenges that such answers may present:

1. In the spirit of 1 Thessalonians 5:21, "Test everything; retain what is good," one needs to analyze the religious traditions of our assemblies to learn how to distinguish the positive elements from the negative ones

2. In the spirit of *Marialis Cultus* (30 and 37), the word of God must be the criterion *par excellence* in developing a valid popular piety. Reliance on sacred Scripture leads to the criteria of faith and witness, so that popular piety may be oriented properly. The official *Book of Blessings* is a magnificent source along these lines; in it, blessings are to include both texts of the Scriptures and a prayer text that calls the faithful to a deep commitment to the Lord

3. In the spirit of the Second Vatican Council, there must be liturgical criteria that can help develop celebrations that may incorporate elements of popular piety such as those witnessed by the historical traditions of Latin America (e.g., when the Feast of Our Lady of Guadalupe falls on a Sunday of Advent). The use of symbols appropriate for the liturgy need not be substituted for others; the inclusion of other symbols, when done tastefully, can enhance our eucharistic celebrations and engage the assembly into a deeper celebration of the Paschal Mystery.

4. In the spirit of post-conciliar documents such as Pope Paul VI's 1975 apostolic exhortation *Evangelii Nuntiandi* (*On Evangelization in the Modern World*), one must analyze anthropological criteria that can aid in the understanding of the inevitable pluralism that surrounds us. We have to consider the mobility of our people in the United States and the developing stages of our Catholics' popular piety as valid manifestations of a socio-cultural setting that cries for a pedagogy of rites and symbols that speak to their unique situation. Our pastoral agents must constantly reevaluate the faithful that gather to celebrate the Lord's mysteries in their specific community at all levels: socioeconomic, cultural, spiritual, and liturgical.

CONCLUSION

Eucharist and the popular piety of the faithful seem to stand as two complimentary—not contradictory—forms of spiritual nourishment for the faithful, particularly among Hispanic Catholics. In history, both forms were perceived as separate and, thus, distant from the core of any Catholic ritual, the celebration of the Paschal Mystery. With Vatican II and its calling for reform, they seem to provide a focus for authentic worship.

While all devotion must lead to the liturgy in its awareness and love of Jesus himself, devotions can become valid manifestations of the transforming power of the traditions[7] that lead many to the Paschal Mystery. This is particularly the case of those who do not have direct contact with parish families or specific worshipping communities but who long to express their faith in ways peculiar to their cultural families. In processions, they can be special offerings of candles or flowers. At pilgrimages or during those key moments of the liturgical year that celebrate either the redemptive work of the Lord or his incarnation in human flesh, the faithful have learned to celebrate their own passage from darkness to light, from sin to grace, and from slavery to freedom. Popular piety, at those times, through its rituals and symbols, has become their doorway to personal and communal liberation.

Questions for Reflection

1. As we consider our worshipping assembly in this community or parish, what religious cultural elements can we identify? Which of these elements or symbols are common to all and which are distinctly different?

2. How would we describe popular piety in our community or parish family?

3. At which moments of the liturgical year can we incorporate some elements of popular piety as a form of expression of the assembly and as a doorway to evangelizing those who otherwise do not gather weekly with the community?

[1] Zuern, SJ, Theodore, "The Preservation of Native Identity in the Process of Inculturation, as Experienced in American Indian Cultures" *On Being Church in a Modern Society* (Rome: Pontifical Gregorian University, 1983).

[2] Pope Benedict XVI describes these words magnificently in his 2006 encyclical *Deus caritas est.*

[3] See among other articles: Sosa, Juan, "An Anglo-Hispanic Dilemma: Liturgical Piety or Popular Piety?" *Liturgy*, vol. 23, no. 6, p. 7–9, and "Liturgy and Popular Piety, a Marriage Made on Earth," *Church*, vol. 15, no. 3, p. 13–16.

[4] Clearly a basic theme in Pope Paul VI's apostolic exhortation *On Evangelization in the Modern World*, (*Evangelii Nuntiandi*) (1975), par. 48.

[5] Papal Documents: Pius X's motu propio *Tra Le Sollicitudini* (1903); Pius XII's *Mediator Dei* (1947), and Pope Paul VI's *Marialis Cultus* (1974).

[6] Latin American Conference of Catholic Bishops, *Puebla and Beyond* (New York: Orbis Books, 1979).

[7] Jesuit Cardinal Avery Dulles highlighted this aspect in "Liturgy and Tradition: A Theologian's Perspective," *Antiphon: A Journal for Liturgical Renewal*, 3:1 (1998), p. 9.

SUNDAY CELEBRATION OF THE EUCHARIST IN OUR HISPANIC ASSEMBLIES

A reflection for the Catholic Common Ground Initiative: a personal journey and a journey with others in the Instituto Nacional Hispano de Liturgia

I shared the following reflections at the gathering held by the Catholic Common Ground Initiative in the fall of 1999 in Los Angeles, California. I try to blend some aspects of my personal journey with that of my ministry and the persistent journey of the many members of the Instituto Nacional Hispano de Liturgia on its twentieth anniversary.

I am grateful for the opportunity to share with you these thoughts, which encompass many of my previous reflections on this and similar topics that affect our pastoral life in the United States. Ours is an age of transitions and, as such, an age of vibrant, dynamic opportunities that at times, one must admit, can lead to peculiar mistakes or limitations. Nonetheless, I certainly feel very optimistic and hopeful about this era, for as I have lived through many transitions, I have always experienced both the tensions of the changes involved and the richness of their resolution. Allow me, then, to share with you some personal remarks regarding this age of transition before I delve more concisely on the question of Hispanic Catholics and Sunday Eucharist. I share my experiences with you merely to illustrate a story that may be similar to many others in the country, or even to some in this room. I believe that in the story itself, one may uncover both the tensions of the era in which we live and the ever-present guidance of the Spirit who helps us transform it for the good of others.

A PERSONAL JOURNEY

At age 14, I asked my parents to send me to the United States, as I could no longer share in the joy of the Cuban revolution. It had so drastically changed from its origin and its promises: there was an abolition of Catholic and private education, my pastor and my teachers were expelled, lack of trust permeated among friends and even family members. Several of my closest friends left the country without saying good-bye. I could no longer find a happy place in my native land.

In October of 1961, I experienced my first transition and my first culture shock as I began life in the United States. One year later, I began my seminary studies at St. John Vianney Minor Seminary in Miami, Florida, and experienced my second culture shock. There were two hundred of "them" (Anglo seminarians) and ten of "us" (Hispanic adolescents or young adults, mostly of Cuban ancestry). I became grateful to those of them who reached out to us and angry at those who rejected us and laughed at us because we were different. This subtle, though persistent, animosity did not only come from the students. Once, I remember well, the vice rector called me to his room to inform me: "Juan, you better tell the others that, if they persist in speaking Spanish, they may be expelled." "How strange a statement," I thought, "coming from a brilliant man who understood and spoke almost eleven languages!"

As an extern or adjunct professor who teaches at the same seminary, I walk today through the same hallways and look at the same walls and remember the same rooms and smile a bit to myself when I think, "What would Father think now? I'm here teaching in Spanish and English, in the same seminary that almost kicked us out thirty years ago, and most of today's students are Latinos. What a transition!"

In those days, ordination to the priesthood seemed far off, ten years. Would I make it? The melodies of Gregorian chant and the seminary discipline blended gracefully in my creative life to provide the security I lost when I left Cuba. While I waited for my parents to arrive (they finally did, six years later), Mother Church nurtured me and assured me that I was on the right track. I enjoyed the sports; the discussions among ourselves; our dreams and hopes; our occasional, and more tolerated, display of Caribbean music at seminary; "Gaudeamuses," the two high Masses at which we sang during the week; and music class, which provided me with the foundation for all my musical expertise.

We watched the 1962 opening of the Second Vatican Council on television in a delayed transmission from Rome and, foolishly, looked for our bishop in the entrance procession. We cried when President Kennedy died and prayed the rosary together in the seminary chapel, all two hundred of us. We even witnessed the death of Lee Harvey Oswald on live television. We saw our older friends move to the major seminary in Boynton Beach and longed to see the day when we, too, could graduate from classical Latin and Greek to philosophy and theology. We heard of former seminarians joining the army and going to Vietnam and, not too many months later, we heard of their deaths. In the middle of it all, we walked together through the reforms of Vatican II as we experienced another transition, another cultural/spiritual shock; not only was the world changing, so was Mother Church!

We had begun to feel some of the Council's changes at the minor seminary, but never as heavily as when we moved to the major one. Drilled in scholastic philosophy, we welcomed with curiosity and excitement new professors with new ideas. The pluralistic basis of the ecumenical council literally blew our minds; this was the time of existentialism in philosophy and hermeneutics in Scripture, the time to explore Kierkegaard and Camus, Nietzsche and Marcel, Barth, Bultmann, Schleiermacher, Otto, Eliade, Rahner, Schillebeeckx and even Pannenberg.

Our goal was now to search, to look for God's compassionate presence in the many and not only in the one way of expression; it was, indeed, an honest intellectual exercise. And as I read *Nostra Aetate* (1965), the last document signed by the Council fathers, I realized that we had begun a new era, for in it I discovered that the Church recognized in anyone who searched for God—Catholic or non-Catholic, baptized or unbaptized—the seeds of faith and truth.[1]

Indeed, we, as a Church, moved on intellectually, but I feel that we forgot to take our people with us, or did not know how to. We could tell through our apostolic work or field education that parish life was becoming far from uniform and straightforward. It was becoming more complex and confusing. Statues had been removed from some sanctuaries, and choirs ceased to sing Gregorian chant as part of their repertoire.

While theologians and members of the hierarchy had been prepared for the Council from the beginning of the twentieth century (at least, since the 40s and 50s), the faithful did not seem to be prepared at all. More transition and changes brought more tensions. The religious community that ran our major seminary did not have enough personnel to manage it any more. They left after our ordination to the deaconate, and we spent the last year of our seminary formation with a totally new faculty, acquired from other seminaries around the country. They were mostly elderly priests for whom the reforms of the Council were not as important as the *Denzinger* manual, another transition. This shift, however, was drastic and detrimental to my classmates, but we needed to hang-in there for only eight more months, and we did. We were happily ordained in 1972 and most of us are still priests in various dioceses in Florida. Shortly after this transition, I learned to trust more in God. I learned to focus not so much on problems, but on possibilities and resolutions.

My first few years in the priesthood were both enriching and painful. Our diocese was changing. More Hispanics were joining it and their needs became more evident. Most of our non-Hispanic clergy did not understand this influx of new people from another country and resented the intrusion of immigrants who called themselves an exiled community. Our parishes were changing and our lives were changing.

While I served as Associate Director of Religious Education for the Archdiocese in the late 1970s, I was introduced to a group of people who wanted to start a national liturgical institute. We met at the Mexican American Cultural Center (MACC) in San Antonio, Texas, and, since then, my involvement in the liturgical life of Hispanic Catholics has not ceased. It becomes important to always note the ongoing efforts of the Mexican American Cultural Center. Likewise, to acknowledge the efforts of other pastoral institutes to identify and address issues that have been critical to Hispanic Catholics in the United States. They all strive to bring the Gospel of Jesus to these communities at all levels of experience by using all available resources in a language and a culture familiar to them.

This year, the Instituto Nacional Hispano de Liturgia[2] will celebrate its twentieth anniversary after undergoing many transitions and after walking with our bishops, our clergy and religious, our committed laity and seminarians through many changes. The Instituto was born out of two major needs: to assist the bishops of the country in their mandate to carry out the liturgical reforms of Vatican II and as a means of exploring and projecting the future inculturation of the Roman liturgy among Hispanic Catholic assemblies.[3]

A JOURNEY WITH OTHERS: MISSION AND MINISTRY

Instituto members came from all parts of the United States; they were Hispanic pastoral agents with not much influence in their dioceses or parishes, but with a great deal of spirituality and love of Church, which many find extraordinary. I witnessed their gifts and talents surface during my presidency in the organization, while I still coordinated the deaconate program in my archdiocese and, later on, the office of worship and spiritual life.

I saw their dedication and loyalty in action during the 1985 Encounter and during many other national gatherings of Hispanic leaders. I have used many of their ideas as a pastor in South Florida. In short, I have been enriched spiritually and personally by my interaction with Hispanic liturgists throughout the country. They are not too loud or outspoken, but they bring to the Church a sense of the sacred, a love of the Eucharist, and much dedication to the Church. If I speak, then, about Sunday Eucharist from the context of our Hispanic Catholics, I do it within the overall context of our journeys as an Instituto: from San Antonio to Los Angeles, Chicago, New York, Miami, Houston, Albuquerque, Orlando, San Jose, Seattle and many other cities and rural areas of the country.

The uniqueness of the Instituto's journey lies in its focus. Neither ideological platforms nor political demonstrations have necessarily accompanied Hispanic liturgists in their commitment to the double task of liturgical renewal and the exploration of liturgical inculturation. They have shared the need to explicate the mystery of God in the lives of people undergoing enormous social changes that affect their value system. The Instituto's journey has focused on the desire to help Hispanics pray at their best—particularly at Sunday Eucharist—even when their life experiences reflect the worst circumstances.

During 1982, the Instituto studied the structure of the Mass among representative Hispanic communities in the United States.[4] The Bishops' Committee on the Liturgy (now called the USCCB Secretariat for Divine Worship) had commissioned this study and challenged the Instituto, in collaboration with the Federation of Diocesan Liturgical Commissions (FDLC), to assess the range of Hispanic responses to current liturgical reforms. The project began on the very eve of the twentieth anniversary of Vatican II's promulgation of the Constitution on the Sacred Liturgy, *Sacrosanctum Concilium*. Thus, the Instituto faced a new and important transition, one that would actively engage its members in the Church's efforts to fulfill the Council's mandate to form pastoral agents in the reforms of the Roman liturgy and to study the adaptation of the liturgy to the various traditions of the faithful:

> Even in the liturgy, the Church has no wish to impose a rigid uniformity in matters which do not implicate the faith or the good of the whole community; rather does she respect and foster the genius and talents of the various races and peoples. ...Sometimes, in fact she admits such things into the liturgy itself, so long as they harmonize with its true and authentic spirit.[5]

This study's random sample of Hispanic attitudes provided an initial step in the greater tasks still ahead, not just for Hispanic communities but for all communities involved in liturgical renewal. A cultural adaptation of the liturgy in the United States may emerge, if at all, only when all recognize the unique contributions of the various cultural groups that participate in the worship of the Catholic Church in this country. It now certainly surfaces in multicultural celebrations.

Instituto members arranged to translate the instrument known as the *Mystery of Faith* into Spanish and developed a catechetical tool known as *Tomen y Coman*. They also worked on a parish process to assess the key elements that Hispanic Catholics value at Sunday worship as well as other elements they might like to see included in the future if the process of inculturation was to take place. In essence, two basic questions emerged to confront the participants: First, how do Hispanics see their own culture already being incorporated into the eucharistic liturgy of the Church? Second, how can elements of their cultural background enhance the richness of the Roman liturgical tradition?

The first question helped participants realize that the mandate of Jesus to celebrate the Eucharist contains key elements that are especially appealing to Hispanics throughout the world because they are also intrinsic to Hispanic culture. Jesus' mandate presses us to seek a more personal style of celebration[6] and a more spontaneous avenue for community expression. Hispanics especially need to share both words and symbols at their deepest level. They feel a collective imperative to celebrate life despite oppression and helplessness, and they share a common desire to continue to celebrate God's gifts of love in the Lord even after the formal structure of the celebration has ended.

The second question stimulated the participants to contribute positively to the liturgical reform of the Church from their own experiences. This question dealt primarily with the issue of cultural adaptation, a prerequisite for exploring liturgical inculturation.[7] The variety of responses clustered under this heading reflected the participants' evaluation of the structure of the Mass from various angles: the celebrant, other ministers, the style of music and texts, the dimensions of art and environment, and the time required to listen to the Lord and to celebrate his banquet of love.

The results were remarkable. About seven hundred Hispanics of Mexican American, Puerto Rican, Cuban, and other ethnic backgrounds constituted the random sample in this process. Representing about sixty parishes in the nation, these groups expressed a tremendous interest in the study of the Mass. Moreover, their gifts and needs in relation to the eucharistic liturgy provided a common base for unity, rather than division, as their hunger for God's word and sacrament became more real throughout the sessions. Today, the study continues as a form of liturgical catechesis in those communities that still use it. It also serves to provide a balance in the understanding of the two basic elements of Vatican II's liturgical reform, tradition and creativity.[8]

> Christian faith is incarnational, rooted in the cultures of people called to experience the presence of the Lord. It is communitarian, tied to almost 2,000 years of permanency yet ever-dynamic for those, bound to Jesus, who turn to each other in the service of charity. Thus, Christian faith also reflects a social dimension: it challenges the community to meet the needs of others, especially the weakest among its neighbors.... As Christian faith is rooted in tradition, it remains open to growth and creativity in its expression.[9]

Almost unanimously, the participants of this widespread study made liturgical music their first priority in cultural adaptation. Hispanics preferred melodies and rhythms interpreted with local instruments rather than with some of the more traditional instruments used in worship.

Secondly, Hispanics perceive the eucharistic liturgy as a dynamic and moving prayer, and they resent the extremes of either being rushed through it or experiencing this prayer from a very static viewpoint. For this reason, they recommend the incorporation of gestures and movements that would draw them more deeply into the mysteries they are celebrating, especially at the entrance procession, the

Gospel procession, the presentation of the gifts, and/or the recessional. They assert that more visual aids are necessary to provide a clear focus on Church tradition. They want to encourage the development of liturgical art and audiovisual tools to energize the Liturgy of the Word.

Thirdly, participants in the study pointed out the importance of those ministers[10] who preside or who exercise specific functions within the celebration. Groups respectfully called for celebrants with a more personal touch; for deacons and readers with clearer diction and better delivery of God's word; for music ministers well trained both in the tradition of Church music and in the musical traditions of their culture; and for key Hispanic diocesan personnel who could deal with these issues at a diocesan level rather than merely as volunteers.

Fourth, but not least important, was the issue of texts. Good texts in Spanish, accessible to our people's understanding and proclaimed well, needed to surface so that Sunday worship could truly become a prayerful experience at which all could participate fully. Since this study, the efforts that produced the *Texto Único*[11] and the elaboration of rituals, even of the upcoming Spanish *Sacramentario* (*El Misal Romano*), by the (BCL's) Subcommittee on Liturgy for Hispanics, began as responses to the needs expressed by these pleas.[12]

As a pastor and as a diocesan director of an office of worship, I must concur with these needs and recommendations. For these four elements—music, gesture and movement, formation of ministers, and elaboration of texts—continue to surface as the key ingredients that need attention at Sunday worship among these Hispanic communities. Since this study at subsequent gatherings of Instituto members and other groups, the following concerns about Sunday Eucharist, among others, have emerged out of the shared, ongoing reflection of Instituto members and friends with their own constituency at the local level:

1. The need for better training of liturgical ministers at all levels, particularly local musicians, so that better Hispanic-US liturgical music may be composed and our assemblies may not need to rely so heavily on Spanish music produced in other countries (e.g., Spain)

2. More clarity and education on the distinction between liturgical music (to be used at the celebration of the sacraments and other liturgical celebrations) and radio or Christian music, which serves as a source of inspiration to individuals and groups at other prayerful moments

3. The exploration of gesture and movement at more Sunday celebrations

4. The quick and, at times, out-of-focus nature of the introductory rites (joy or penance, interior disposition or praise?)

5. The need for good silence at appropriate times, since the language of silence greatly enhances the assembly's contemplation of the celebrated mysteries

6. The involvement of youth at liturgical celebrations and the importance of dress codes among those in the assembly and unified posture among liturgical ministers who sit in the sanctuary

7. The brevity of the concluding rite, which Hispanics do not mind extending at times, if such an extension includes varied and specific forms of blessings (i.e., *Book of Blessings*); for the most part, Hispanic assemblies enjoy extended blessings toward the end of Mass, after which they continue to share fellowship outside of the liturgical space

8. Liturgical catechesis on the actual forms of distribution of the Eucharist in the United States, which many Hispanic clergy and laity who come from other Spanish-speaking countries to serve in the United States simply do not know, as they have been guided by different liturgical legislation

9. The analysis and exploration of the symbolic language of our Hispanics' popular piety vis-à-vis its possible incorporation into the liturgy. While maintaining the Roman rite intact, and without doing injustice to it, certain aspects of Marian themes may be inserted into a Sunday celebration at specific times of the year (e.g., the feast of Our Lady of Guadalupe or other titles of Our Lady that are special to the community that celebrates)[13]

10. The reality of bilingual and bicultural celebrations, how to prepare them, how and when to introduce the entire assembly to them, and the role of the pastor vis-à-vis these celebrations.

GUIDING PRINCIPLES AT WORSHIP IN HISPANIC CATHOLIC ASSEMBLIES

What guides our journey of transitions in which, on one side, we wish to serve our people well while, on the other, we are confronted by multiple tensions that seek some type of pastoral resolution? Allow me now to share with you some of the principles and/or criteria that guide our reflections as pastors, catechists, and liturgists committed to Hispanic ministry in the United States. They are based primarily on the interaction between the study of liturgy and the *sensus fidelium* in this country, particularly of Hispanic assemblies.

A. The liturgical reform always aimed primarily at the renewal of the faithful.

Cardinal Jean Villot would remind participants at CELAM's[14] encounter of diocesan liturgical commissions of Latin America of this principle through his historic letter of 1977.[15] In it, he delineated the five major criteria on which this renewal is to take place: full and active participation; the use of the vernacular languages at worship; the rediscovery of God's word and its use at all liturgical celebrations; the formation and development of liturgical ministers; and the openness to cultural adaptations of the liturgy.

Hispanic liturgists in the United States continue to work hard at making the Council reforms truly become what they were meant to be from the beginning: an expression of the renewal of the people, and not vice versa. The external reforms must flow from the spiritual renewal of the faithful; when such a process is absent, the results may be disastrous. Instituto members long to see Sunday worship as a more incarnated reality in the lives of the people, while maintaining that necessary balance between tradition and creativity at its foundation. When we lose the sense of the sacred, we open the door to mediocrity. When creativity or the capacity and willingness for adaptation disappears, we embrace once again theological and liturgical reductionism; we become stagnant. Neither option has anything to do with transitions; it has a lot to do with spirituality.

B. In the United States, where most urban centers have evolved into multicultural communities, Sunday worship must first consider the anthropological principle of integration before considering that of inculturation,[16] which flows from the principle known as cultural adaptation, as enunciated by *Sacrosanctum Concilium.*[17]

Let us briefly recall: in their NCCB-USCC (now the USCCB) document *Cultural Pluralism in the United States,*[18] as well as in the *Pastoral Letter for Hispanics*[19], the bishops of our country reject the melting pot theory, which makes it impossible for individuals to maintain their cultural heritage and identity while attempting to participate actively in the social life of the country. The American bishops opt for cultural pluralism, which allows for a mosaic of cultures and the possibility for all pilgrim communities to live together and contribute to the larger society while maintaining their own roots and traditions, in essence, a new ethnicity, a *mestizaje.*[20]

If inculturation is the process by which each person assimilates his/her own culture, and if transculturation describes the interaction among cultural groups that coexist particularly in heavily-populated urban centers, integration, then, describes the process by which cultural groups meet and constitute themselves. They do not exist in opposition with one another but, rather, as a mosaic of cultural families, capable of exchanging specific and unique traits among themselves and of influencing each other in the process.[21]

Three criteria become essential for any community or assembly to embrace this process of integration. First, there is the belief that diversity is not a threat but a gift. Second, the criterion of cultural selectivity, which maintains that cultural groups will select the intensity of their involvement with new lifestyles and will accept new cultural traits from a more dominant group, depending on how those traits conform to their preexistent traits and style of living. And third, the need for cultural groups to experience liminal or pseudo-liminal moments by which they can be in touch with their own roots and the symbols and myths that have fashioned them and that identify them uniquely as who they are.[22]

In this context, Hispanic Catholics appear to feel more at home as they remember the rich mythology of their traditions and celebrate the multifaceted rituals that sustain that mythology. Indeed, it has been ascertained that through liturgy and the celebration of popular religious rituals, they begin to experience a sense of liberation from the ordinary rhythm of life with its many crises. The truth remains: if we as Church are not aware of this process or fail to support their search, they will turn to pseudo-liminal experiences outside the Catholic tradition to reach inner peace as well as social adaptation in our complex society.[23]

C. Whereas Sunday worship and popular piety may always remain distinct,[24] they, together, can also constitute a unique form of prayer in the spiritual journey of our Hispanic Catholic families. For Hispanic Catholics in the United States, popular piety—infused with God's word and properly nurtured—can become the language of (or an avenue toward) both the reforms of the Council and the inculturation of the liturgy.[25] At this point, allow me to summarize this principle by quoting from *El Cuerpo de Cristo*, a recent publication that contains the papers presented at a Symposium on Hispanic Liturgy held at Catholic University in May 1997.

The U.S. Church, through our Hispanic Catholics, is witnessing an ongoing tension that requires attention and focus. In the dialogue between liturgy and popular religiosity, we need to perceive other ongoing dialogues that should become part of the pastoral life of the Church in a more serious way. We need to address the broader dialogue between faith and culture that calls for a reinterpretation of our pastoral life in light of the needs of the people and not of our own needs, as structured by previous experiences not present today. Secondly, we also need to enter into the dialogue between our Catholic culture and non-Christian cultures still prevalent in the religious symbolism of our Hispanic Catholics, who, in turn, come from areas of Latin America in which several cultures and non-Christian religious practices prevail, some of Native American ancestry, others, of African roots.[26]

Popular religiosity (piety) and liturgy—rather than remaining opposed and distant elements of our pastoral life—can become for us the avenue through which we can reinterpret those stories and symbols that shape the Hispanic worldview. I venture to propose that, for Hispanic Catholics, this pastoral gift constitutes the path to the new evangelization in which the living Gospel of Jesus Christ reaches those who search for good news in our culture of death.

CONCLUSION

The age of transitions continues and it will not stop. The more our global communication develops and we accept the challenge of knowing one another worldwide, the more we will come to know others' viewpoints and interpretations of reality. How are we to react? I hope that our response is, as Jesus would have reacted, with respect for the other, an openness to love the person—though one may disagree with the other's propositions—and a willingness to grow and mature through sharing and dialogue. May the Father of all, who sent his Son to rescue us from petty divisions and sin, continue to breathe his Spirit on our efforts to serve God's people with compassion and love as we endeavor to celebrate our one faith, from our common baptism, in and through the Lord of all!

---

[1] Walter M. Abbot, S.J., "Declaration on the Relationship of the Church to Non-Christian Religions," *The Documents of Vatican II*. (New York: The American Press, 1966), paragraph 2.

[2] In 2008, the Instituto celebrates its twenty-ninth anniversary

[3] The constitution of the Instituto Nacional Hispano de Liturgia clearly delineates this double purpose in its first pages. The Instituto has a permanent office at The Catholic University of America in Washington, DC.

[4] For a more complete description of this project, read Juan J. Sosa. "Let us Pray . . . en Español," *Liturgy, Journal of the Liturgical Conference*, vol. 3, no. 2, pp. 63–67. It also appears in *Notitiae*, 219, vol. 20 (1984), pp. 68–696.

[5] "Constitution on the Sacred Liturgy," par. 37.

[6] "Personal" does not mean "improvised" or "colloquial;" it means accessible, respectful of the tradition shared and engaging with the assembly.

[7] Since then, the Congregation for Divine Worship and the Discipline of the Sacraments released its *Fourth Instruction on the Roman Liturgy and Inculturation, Varietates Legitimae,* in January 1994.

[8] Jesuit Cardinal Avery Dulles addresses this balance in particular in his essay "Liturgy and Tradition: A Theologian's Perspective," *Antiphon*, 3:1 (New Hope, KY: Society for Catholic Liturgy, 1998), 4–11, 20.

[9] Juan J. Sosa, "The Ministry of Liturgical Music among Hispanic Communities," in *Liturgy 80* (Chicago: Office for Divine Worship of the Archdiocese of Chicago, October 1981), p. 12.

[10] Whereas *Sacrosanctum Concilium* called for the establishment of more liturgical ministers in paragraphs 28–32, the roles of these ministers were not fully developed until the 2000 revision of the *Ordo Missae* and the 2004 publication of *Redemptionis Sacramentum.*

[11] For a complete reference to this unified text in Spanish, please see *Notitiae*, n. 236/237. This text was reached first as a translation of *De Benedictionibus* and, consequently, of the *Ordo Missae* by all Spanish-speaking countries of the world. For a synthesis of how these national bodies reached a consensus on one translation, please see Juan J. Sosa's "*Texto Único*: A Unified Liturgical Text for Spanish-speaking Catholics." *Liturgia y Canción* (Portland, OR: Oregon Catholic Press, vol. 1, no. 1, pp. 5–8.

[12] It is to be noted that other ritual books have been approved by the bishops of the country for use by Spanish-speaking communities, most recently *El Rito del Bautismo, El Rito del Matrimonio,* and *El Ritual de la Quinceañera* (the latter confirmed by Rome).

[13] Some suggestions: the location of the venerated image on one side of the sanctuary, references to the feast during the homily and prayers for the specific community during the prayer of the faithful, an offering of flowers during the presentation of the gifts, and the use of music appropriate for the occasion.

[14] CELAM translates this as the International Bishops' Conference of Latin America. The Instituto maintains periodic communication with its department of liturgy, as well as the liturgy departments of the Bishops' Conference of Mexico, Spain, and Argentina.

[15] See "La Renovación Litúrgica en América Latina," *Revista Medellín*, vol. 3, no. 12, Diciembre de 1977.

[16] For a good description of inculturation, see, among others, Anscar J. Chupungco, OSB, *Cultural Adaptation of the Liturgy* (New York: Paulist Press, 1982), and John Mary Waliggo, "Making a Church that is Truly African" in *Inculturation: Its meaning and Urgency* (Nairobi, Kenya: St. Paul Publications in Africa, 1986).

[17] Paragraphs 37–40 of the Constitution describe the essence of the principle of cultural adaptation. For a more explicit display of this principle, please read Juan J. Sosa's "Renewal and Inculturation" in *Liturgy: A Journal of the Liturgical Conference*, vol. 9, no. 2 (Winter 1990), pp. 17–27.

[18] "Cultural Pluralism in the United States," by the USCC Committee for Social Development and World Peace in *Origins*, 10:31 (Washington, DC: USCCB Publishing, January 15, 1981).

[19] *The Hispanic Presence: Challenge and Commitment: A Pastoral Letter on Hispanic Ministry* (Washington, DC: USCCB Publishing, 1983).

[20] See Virgil Elizondo's doctoral thesis as well as his writings on this theme.

[21] See the publications by Melville Herskovits, especially *Man and His Works* (New York: Alfred A. Knopf, 1967), pp. 300–302.

[22] Beside the original work of Arnold Van Gennep in *The Rites of Passage* (Chicago: University of Chicago Press, 1961), the work of Victor Turner is crucial to understand the concept of liminality. See, among others, *The Ritual Process* (Chicago, IL: Aldine Publishing Co., 1969), *Drama, Fields, and Metaphors* (Ithaca, NY: Cornell University Press, 1974), and *The Forest of Symbols* (Ithaca, NY: Cornell University Press, 1967).

[23] Many references can be found in contemporary society about Pentecostal gatherings constituted by Hispanics who were previously Catholic, as well as about gatherings of religious syncretisms, such as *Santería, Spiritism*, the New Age, and other sects and cults.

[24] See "Pope John Paul II on Popular Piety and Liturgy." *Bishops' Committee on the Liturgy Newsletter*, vol. XXII, June/July, 1986.

[25] Indeed, a clear axiom in *Evangelii Nuntiandi*, Pope Paul VI, *Apostolic Exhortation on Evangelization in the Modern World*, (December 8, 1975), paragraph 48.

[26] Juan J. Sosa, "Hispanic Liturgy and Popular Religiosity," *El Cuerpo de Cristo*, (New York: The Crossroad Publishing Company, 1998), p. 74.

LITURGICAL TEXTS FOR SPANISH-SPEAKING CATHOLICS OF THE UNITED STATES
An essay on the Spanish texts in use for the US and the development of future texts for our liturgical assemblies

As a member of the Bishops' Committee on the Liturgy's Subcommittee for Hispanics, I was asked by the editors of Liturgia y Canción *by Oregon Catholic Press to summarize, in an essay, the issue of texts in Spanish. I have tried to do so in the following reflections, while updating some of their contents as a result of more recent directives and expected future publications in Spanish.*

For decades now, our Catholic leadership in the United States has been wondering about Spanish texts for our Catholic assemblies. What texts can be used? Are they different from those published by the Bishops' Conferences of Spain and/or Latin America? Which are most appropriate? Are there different ways of speaking Spanish? Can there actually be one and the same text for all Hispanics in the country?

Hispanic priests had begun to deal with this issue as an initial response to the liturgical reforms of Vatican II when, in Miami and in New York in the late sixties and early seventies, the then new (1969) "Ordinary of the Mass" for Spanish-speaking Catholics was printed in small but handy publications with selected songs appropriate to the reformed liturgy.

The issue was again addressed in the mid-seventies at the Mexican-American Cultural Center in San Antonio, Texas, when members of the pastoral staff began to explore the possibility of printing bilingual rituals to help English-speaking priests who served Hispanic communities, as well as Hispanic priests and deacons themselves. It was there and then, in 1979, that the Instituto de Liturgia Hispana was born to assist the bishops of our country in all matters of liturgy and spirituality for Hispanic Catholics. Shortly afterwards the Subcommittee for Hispanics of the Bishops' Committee on the Liturgy was established by the bishops themselves specifically to deal with this issue of Spanish texts for the United States. The Subcommittee continues to address the issue in an effort to assess and to promote, through the BCL (now the USCCB Committee on Divine Worship), the best and most appropriate Spanish texts for our Catholic assemblies, pending the approval of these proposals by the bishops of our country and by the Congregation for Divine Worship and the Sacrament.

Although this article hopes to reply to some of the questions posed in its first paragraph and, to therefore, diminish the apparent anxiety that some of our pastoral agents display in this area, one issue remains clear: Spanish is a language understood by all of our Hispanic Catholic assemblies in the United States, although certain accents and the meaning of certain colloquial words and expressions may differ. The usage of Spanish in the country is similar to the usage of English here and in Great Britain or New Zealand; this is not a case of distinct Asian or Native American languages or dialects, but more one of the same language with distinct local usages.

A BRIEF HISTORICAL OVERVIEW

As reported in our 1989 article on the *Texto Único,*[1] since Vatican II there have only been two major gatherings of liturgical representatives of Spanish-speaking bishops' conferences to address jointly the issue of texts for Spanish-speaking assemblies: 1) the 1964 joint Commission (Spain and CELAM[2]) that worked until 1971 in response to the vernacular needs echoed by Vatican II and that produced the Ordinary of the Mass in Spanish, one for Spain and the other for Latin America, as well as the first set of Mass Propers, almost literally translated from the first *editio typica*; and 2) the 1986 joint Commission, sponsored by the Congregation for Divine Worship, that worked on the common edition of the *Book of Blessings (De Benedictionibus)*. Out of this gathering a new Spanish text for the Ordinary of the Mass (*Ordo Missae*), widely known now as the *Texto Único*, also emerged.

By the time our liturgical representative for the United States, Bishop Ricardo Ramírez, then chairperson for our BCL Subcommittee, and Fr. John Gurrieri, then the BCL's Executive Director, joined the second Commission, Spanish had been approved in 1984 as a liturgical language for the United States[3], and the Subcommittee had been working on the adaptation of various texts approved in Mexico and, subsequently, in this country.

Almost the entire edition of the March/April 1986 edition of *Notitiae*, the official publication of the Roman Congregation for Divine Worship, was dedicated to the historical gathering. In particular, section V of that publication provides interested liturgists with a complete description of the liturgical texts published in all of the Spanish-speaking countries of the world as part of the information report that each country's representatives offered on behalf of their assemblies. Almost every country was represented in this report, from Argentina to Venezuela. The United States report, contained on pages 193 to 197 in twelve numbered paragraphs, becomes quite significant for all of us. It proves we are the fifth largest Spanish-speaking country in the world. The report provides us with criteria, some initial accomplishments, and much needed expectations. In summary:

1. Until ritual texts in Spanish were approved by the U.S. bishops for use in the county, those who presided at liturgical celebrations in Spanish

were permitted to use those liturgical books already approved by the Bishops' Conferences of any Spanish-speaking country in the world

2. The Subcommittee for Hispanics was committed to study the various translations into Spanish of liturgical texts, especially of the Roman Missal, to recommend a common translation for use in this country as well as possible adaptations of other approved texts for the rituals and the integration of special liturgical feasts, celebrated by Hispanic Catholics in the United States, into the particular calendar of the country as an appendix to the final edition of the Roman Missal

3. The following liturgical books were most widely accepted in our parishes (as of that date, February of 1986):

   Roman Missal (from Spain, Mexico, and Colombia)
   Roman Ritual (from Spain, Mexico, and Argentina)
   Roman Pontifical (from Spain and Argentina)
   Roman Lectionary (from the United States and Spain)

4. The first volume of the *Leccionario, Edición Hispanoamericana* was prepared by the Northeast Catholic Center for Hispanics (New York) in 1982. Approved by our Bishops' Conference, this Lectionary used the translation of the Latin American Bible already approved for the Peruvian Lectionary. (Since this time, the Lectionary for Mexico has been voted in and approved as the Lectionary for use in the parishes and communities of the United States. A new published edition of this Spanish Leccionario for the United States is forthcoming, while the Mexican version of these texts continues to appear throughout the country)

5. In cooperation with the Liturgical Secretariat of the Mexican Episcopal Conference, an adapted bilingual version of *Pastoral Care of the Sick* was published for use in this country, particularly by those who used Spanish as a second language, as *Cuidado Pastoral de los Enfermos: Ritos de la Unción y del Viático*

6. In its concluding comments, our representative expressed the interest of all bishops in the United States for maintaining the initiative of this project in future efforts: to continue the joint publication of the best liturgical texts in Spanish for all Spanish-speaking assemblies of the world. In paragraph 11 of the report, he exclaims: "It is our experience in the English-speaking world that a common translation of liturgical texts not only serves to unify the worship of each country,

but also foster common bonds among the countries who use the same language at worship. The work of ICEL, the International Commission of English in the Liturgy, has united the English-speaking world at worship."[4] (Since this time, a new ICEL has been formed under the guidelines provided by *Liturgical Authenticam,* the fifth instruction on vernacular translation of the Roman Liturgy. These guidelines apply not only to the English-speaking world but to all of the vernacular languages used in the Church today.)

THE PRESENT AND FUTURE OF SPANISH TEXTS

On the First Sunday of Advent of 1989, the *Texto Único* became the official Ordinary of the Mass in Spanish for the United States of America. Only those texts approved by the bishops of the country for use at Spanish-speaking assemblies are to be used. Consequently, texts not available through our Bishops' Conference because they are not available or approved yet may be used from other liturgical books approved in other countries until they are approved and published in the United States as the proper books of the Hispanic Catholic assemblies. Two questions may result from these observations: What are the approved texts? And what texts have not been approved yet?

As a result of the proposals of the Subcommittee for Hispanics and the input and commitment of our publishing houses, only the following texts should be in use as approved texts in Spanish for the United States:

1982 *Sunday Lectionary* (*Leccionario Dominical*), published by the Northeast Pastoral Center for Hispanics

1983 *Pastoral Care of the Sick* (*Cuidado Pastoral de los Enfermos*), bilingual edition published by Liturgy Training Publications and the Mexican-American Cultural Center

1988 *Daily Lectionary* (*Leccionario Ferial*), also published by the Northeast Center

1989 *Ordinario de la Misa,* published in the United States by the Catholic Book Publishing Company

1991 *RICA* (*Ritual de la Iniciación Cristiana para Adultos*), published by Liturgy Training Publications.

1994 *Sunday Celebrations in the Absence of a Priest* (*Celebraciones Dominicales en la Ausencia de un Presbítero*), bilingual edition published by Liturgical Press

2001 *Order of Christian Funerals* (*El Ritual de las Exequias Cristianas*), a full version in Spanish and a bilingual version with selected chapters published by Liturgical Press in 2002

In 2005, the U.S. Bishops' Conference approved three new rituals in Spanish for use in the diocese of the United States: the *Rite of Baptism* (*El Ritual del Bautismo de Niños*) and the *Rite of Marriage* (*El Ritual del Matrimonio*). These texts need to be confirmed by the Holy See before they are released for publication. The newly fashioned *Ritual de Quinceañeras* has been confirmed by the Holy See.

What about the psalms? These have been taken from the rich version of the Spanish *Liturgy of the Hours* and have been inserted not only in the Lectionaries but also in the ritual books themselves. Apparently, a revision of the translations of these psalms seems to be currently in progress by the Bishops' Conference of Spain.

The work of the *Sacramentario* (*The Roman Missal*), a labor of love and 'details' of almost fifteen years that parallels the U.S. Sacramentary, appears to be almost ready for approval by the bishops. Pending is their review of the third edition of the *General Instruction of the Roman Missal*, released in Rome in the spring of 2001, approved by the Latin members of the United States Catholic Conference in November of 2002, and confirmed by the Congregation for Divine Worship and the Discipline of the Sacraments in 2003. Its impact, however, will serve to stimulate a renewed catechesis on the liturgy among Hispanic Catholics who received little or no catechesis immediately after the Second Vatican Council.

Other texts, not developed yet by our bishops, seem to prevail in many parishes of our country: from the 1983 edition of the *Book of the Chair* (*Libro de la Sede*) from Spain to the Lectionaries from Mexico (1992), the Spanish version of the *Ceremonial of Bishops*, published by CELAM (1991), the Spanish *OCF* (*Exequias*) and the 1994 edition of the revised *Rite of Marriage*.

Attention, however, must be given once again to the original criteria which gave birth to the 1984 decision making Spanish a liturgical language of the United States Catholic communities: as long as the texts have neither been approved nor published in the country, these may be used at random; however, once the texts have become part of the textual heritage of our Church and of our parishes, only these should be used (I am referring mostly to the Lectionaries, *Exequias*, and the upcoming publications of the new rituals of baptism, matrimony and quinceañeras)[5].

REFLECTIONS AND CONCLUSION

Why pay so much attention to liturgical texts? Are they not merely nicely bound books (sometimes falling apart) that are kept on bookshelves in the sacristies for use by priests, deacons, and readers? Do our people actually pay attention to the prayers when they are proclaimed by the presider? Is language so important?

While, unfortunately, many of our people—sometimes our own pastoral leaders—feel that way, we need to focus on liturgical texts from various angles: 1) from the perspective of the crucial principle enunciated by the liturgical reform, namely, "conscious and active participation" (*Sacrosanctum Concilium*, 14); 2) from the insertion of the vernacular as a diverse element of liturgical prayer and a reflection of the diverse communities that constitute our Catholic assemblies today; 3) from the inherent need to preserve the treasure of the euchological texts of the Church (the prayers that have shaped our worship and, I dare say, our lives for almost two thousand years); and even 4) from the perspective of liturgical inculturation that may give birth to new forms of linguistic expressions in the future.

While much has been written and taught about conscious and active participation by the faithful, much more must continue to surface in our local communities, which at times seem to respond poorly to this principle[6]. The language of our assemblies—the vernacular—as a cultural vehicle, must find ways of speaking of and to God, in fidelity to the original Latin proposed by the Church and, thus, emerging out of the tradition of our Church, but which appears adapted to current times with poetic beauty and creative strength. The issue of liturgical language is an issue of preserving and communicating the best of our tradition and the best of our language styles so that the people may find in us an instrument to the mystery of God-among-us, the Holy One we attempt to unveil before them today as many others did in the past[7].

Not many of our presiding ministers can improvise good texts. For the most part, they have neither been trained in poetry nor do they have the time to develop a poetic stand that would make them free to improvise well at liturgical celebrations. In a way, we can admit that we cannot proclaim the Mass prayers, the formulae for the Sacraments, the prefaces and eucharistic prayers, and not even our blessings in the same style we use when we speak with one another, though we may be able to do so at times in sections of the homily. Such prayerful proclamation requires a sacred and yet personal style through which the words of the Church take flesh in the assembly and inspire its members to meet the Lord in praise and thanksgiving. This happens, of course, when we sing. But when we sing out the praises of God, we practice hard to make our singing both clear and beautiful for the sake of worship. Unsung texts deserve the same, if not a more careful, treatment. Nonetheless, our seminary formation must take as seriously as homiletics the aspects of proclamation and singing.

The more we tackle the issue of texts, in this case of Spanish texts, the more we uncover the depth of the liturgical reform. We seem to be confronted not merely with the external use of language, but with the interior disposition of the faithful who long to be in communion with the Lord and who need a symbolic language with which to speak to him in public. We are confronted, indeed, with the renewal of our hearts, the actual focus of the liturgical reform. We are challenged to make this renewal happen in others and to lead them to a joyful way of expressing how alive Christ is in their midst as we, the Church at prayer and song, strive to become the light of the world and the salt of the earth in languages that God can always understand, even if we do not: in English or in Spanish, in Vietnamese or in Polish, in Creole or in Portuguese, in the Pentecost of languages and people that the Lord has entrusted to our care.

---

[1] Sosa, Juan. "Texto Único: A Unified Liturgical Text for Spanish-Speaking Catholics." *Liturgia y Canción.* May/June 1989.

[2] "CELAM" stands for *Conferencia Episcopal Latinoamericana* or Latin American Conference of Bishops.

[3] This decision of our bishops was confirmed by the Holy See by a decree of the Congregation for Divine Worship on January 19, 1985 (Prot. CD 382/384). "Encuentro de las Comisiones Nacionales de Liturgia de Lengua Española organizado por la Congregación para el Culto Divino (Ciudad del Vaticano, 3–7 de febrero de 1986)." *Notitiae*, 236–237, Vol. 22 (1986), Num. 3–4, p. 194.

[4] "Es nuestra experiencia en el mundo de habla inglesa que una traducción común de los textos litúrgicos no solamente unifica el culto de cada país, sino que también fomenta los lazos comunes entre países del mismo idioma. El trabajo de la Comisión Internacional del Inglés en la Liturgia ha unido al mundo de habla inglesa en el culto." Ibid, p. 196.

[5] Most of these texts are published by *Obra Nacional de la Buena Prensa, A.C.*, in Mexico, or by *Coeditores Litúrgicos* in Spain. Even some of the texts proposed and approved by specific bishops' conferences in Latin America are edited and published in Spain.

[6] I have discovered some so-called multicultural celebrations using Latin in substitution for the vernacular and not as an integral component of the celebration. Perhaps, in such cases, those who prepare these liturgies might find it easier to avoid, through the use of Latin instead of diverse vernacular expressions, the ecclesiological issues that lead to multicultural celebrations in today's Church.

[7] A good book to read about this topic is Martimort's *The Church at Prayer (La Iglesia en Oración)*.

LITURGICAL MUSIC IN HISPANIC CATHOLIC ASSEMBLIES OF THE UNITED STATES

A reflection for Hispanic pastoral musicians and their role at the service of the Church in the US

This address was given to the members of Universa Laus who gathered in Connecticut in August 1999 at their annual meeting. Universa Laus is an international organization of liturgical musicians. Some of these reflections were shared in my keynote presentation, "One Body, Many Cultures at Worship" at the 2000 regional convention of the National Association of Pastoral Musicians (NPM) in Orlando, Florida.

It is an honor to participate in this stimulating gathering of liturgical musicians from many parts of the world and to have been selected by the Instituto Nacional Hispano, as its representative in this area of Church life so dear to my heart: liturgical music in our Hispanic Catholic assemblies of the United States. Though I am not a professional or an academic musician, music—specifically liturgical music—has become an inspiration for my pastoral work and the expression of my spiritual journey. I would like to divide my reflections into three parts and provide some samples of the Hispanic liturgical repertoire today; then, I'll offer a few personal conclusions on this topic. The three major sections of my reflections, then, are:

- Music as symbol and prayer
- Hispanic liturgy in the United States
- Spanish liturgical music in Hispanic worship

I thank you for bearing with my melody, rhythm, and text.

MUSIC AS SYMBOL AND PRAYER

Social scientists have assisted bishops, pastors, theologians, liturgists, musicians and, in general, all pastoral agents of the Church to understand the nature and function of symbols in individuals and in cultural groups. These distinctions have been noted by Victor Turner in *The Ritual Process: Structure and Anti-Structure* (Piscataway, NJ: Aldine Transaction, 1995). Religious symbols, either dominant or instrumental, as constitutive to the ritual system of each cultural group, define the group itself that, through its symbols, reveals its values, its priorities, and even the intricacies of its relationships to God and to others. Religious symbols, like other symbols, function in specific ways; as distinct from signs, symbols evoke in the members of a group the deeper reality, which they represent, and they involve them with the depth of that reality and the impact it brings about.

Having heard many eloquent reflections on one of today's most popular terms in Church circles, "inculturation," I cannot help but recall a brief but wonderful article written by Jesuit Father Theodore Zuern and published in 1983 by the Institute on Cultures and Religions of the Pontifical Gregorian University. Titled "The Preservation of Native Identity in the Process of Inculturation, as Experienced in American Indian Cultures," the article provides a set of valuable ideas from which all pastoral agents can profit, whether their pastoral work involves Native Americans, African Americans, Hispanics, or other cultural groups residing in this country and abroad. At the root of these reflections lies the significance of symbolic communication, the essence of culture.

Father Zuern considers culture in a diagram of three concentric circles. A center of intangibles, the first circle, is at the heart of the diagram and represents the meaning level of that culture. This circle includes the culture's myths and symbols, its values and principles, its fundamental questions, and the answers of that culture to those questions. Around the center of intangibles appears the circle of structures, which represents the structures that underlie all the social institutions within a cultural society. These structures, simple or complex as they may be, provide the group with the means to confront and solve the most significant issues about living. These structures are influenced by other circumstances that affect the group, such as the group's history and the environment that surrounds them. The outer circle appears as the circle of tangibles, namely the visible, tangible elements of a culture, those signs and symbols through which the culture finds expression and by which other cultures merely begin to perceive it.

In his article, Father Zuern raises some questions about how we perceive cultures: Is it merely from the outward, outer level, that is, superficially? Or, rather, should we not attempt, at least, to penetrate all levels and come to know the culture from its intangible, non-evident perspective? The answer to this question is significant for all pastoral ministers committed to service in the Church today, particularly for liturgists and musicians, the poets of our post-industrial era who dare transform the intangible reality of the Risen Christ in tangible words, melodies, and songs through which the faithful can come to worship God in community.

I maintain that herein lies the difference between seeing ourselves and others as tourists, merely touching each other's outward layer, or as pilgrims, willing to learn more about one another's thoughts, feelings, and expressions and to respect the differences we discover precisely because we are bonded by a common vision and a common memory that draws us together. I admit, nonetheless, that Father Zuern's simple, yet provocative, thoughts can raise other questions that need answers. As we recall his three concentric circles, we can ask ourselves: where in these circles do we place language?

As we evaluate the language we use in our verbal communication with one another, we uncover a few choices: the language of communication that aims at orienting others on their whereabouts, the economic language of business or the manipulative language of politics, so prevalent in many societies, and the language of myths and symbols that speaks from and to the heart and becomes, in all cultural groups, the language of faith.

We would probably conclude that language must run through all three circles in each culture, although we may insist on preserving certain distinctions. Since Vatican II, we have moved from making our liturgical language one of rubrics and directives. On the other hand, we can neither turn it into the language of business or politics, nor into that of dogma or catechesis. We have been challenged by the liturgical reform to learn to speak the language of God and Church and to express it in simple, yet poetic, ways for contemporary society. What have we actually done with language in the liturgy? What can we do in the future? Do we translate and express texts in the language of tourists, intellectuals, and strangers or have we learned to promote, in our celebrations, the language of pilgrims, a language that leads its listeners to experience the salvific presence of God in history and to long for that presence in sacramental signs? What about music? Where does it belong? Where have we placed it? Where can we place it in the future? Perhaps if we learn to sing in one another's vernacular, we may finally begin to know and love one another better.

Music in Catholic worship is an instrumental symbol, never intended for dominance but for support. Music, however, does not only evoke in worshippers a deeper reality, but also places them in touch with the same reality that has gathered them together. In liturgy, of course, this reality is the Paschal Mystery, the process of dying and rising in Jesus that we have all embraced from the moment of baptism and that we celebrate continually in our pilgrimage to the Father.

In Catholic worship, the reality of the Paschal Mystery assumes diverse features, languages, and styles. Through the liturgy of the global Church, the intangible reality of a God-made and unconditional love in Jesus Christ becomes tangible in the lives and prayers of the communities who share the one Lord and the same faith because of a common baptism. This embrace between the Word and the world's cultures defines the nature of our Catholic community and, simultaneously, challenges us to preserve our unity in faith while celebrating the blessings of the Spirit in diverse forms.

We live in a satellite age where all world events seem to find a way into the minds and hearts of people through various modes of communication. Despite this, we gather to celebrate the presence of our Risen Lord in small communities filled with richness and variety. At communal prayer, when Christians lift up their hearts to the Lord, music echoes the joys, sufferings, hopes, and dreams of the faithful as they blend their voices with the voice of God revealed through biblical texts. At those moments God, as Good News, finds a way into the hearts of his people; more powerful than a satellite made by human hands, he calls them to renewal, reconciliation, compassion, and forgiveness. He calls them to unveil, in tangible ways, the intangible power of his presence.

HISPANIC LITURGY IN THE UNITED STATES

The Catholic Church in the United States enjoys a privileged gift with the presence of a multiplicity of Catholic communities that bring, to the whole of North American Catholicism, the uniqueness of their cultural and religious expressions. Our presentation today, however, must primarily focus on Hispanic worship expressions, specifically music, though I feel that we cannot ignore how much interaction, among all cultural groups, occurs in our complex society each day.

Hispanic Catholics in the United States constitute a composite of cultural traditions that, though rooted historically in the evangelization of the Americas by Spain, has developed, over the centuries, unique characteristics. The Catholic Church in this country has witnessed a display of these characteristics particularly, though not exclusively, in large urban centers where representative families from Mexico, Central, and South America, the Caribbean Islands, and even from Portugal and Spain have settled to become part of the larger, complex North American society, all without losing their unique cultural identity.

Integrated, though not assimilated, these families, who worship in spirit and truth, experience a two-fold dynamic:

- On one side, they fear the disintegration of family values as a result of social strains that lead their youth away from God and Church toward a depressing secularism that markets primarily a spirit of consumerism and relativism

- On the other hand, they wish to express their faith in Jesus, the Church, Mary and the Saints in ways that can help them liberate themselves and their children from those strains and journey to happiness and peace

They live in this country not as tourists, but as pilgrims whose journey of faith and love is positively contagious to other cultural groups and unreservedly catholic in the best possible description of this term. At times, however, and under specific circumstances, they have suffered the misunderstanding and the oppression of specific local groups, even Church leaders, that has led them away from the Church of their initiation into other ecclesial congregations, syncretisms, or sects foreign to their heritage but rich in hospitality and understanding.

The cultural pluralism provided by the Second Vatican Council in its theological renewal and liturgical reforms and the spirit in which the reforms have evolved over years facilitate, for our Hispanic Catholics, a medium in which they can contribute their gifts and talents to the spiritual growth of all Catholics. It is also an opportunity to ensure their own Catholic and cultural identity in the midst of rapid and complex social changes.

From the many elements that comprise the reformed vision of Vatican II and subsequent synods, liturgy and spirituality need to become for all Catholics, in this case Hispanic Catholics living in the United States, the backbone, the fountain from which their lives find meaning and the summit toward which their hearts must journey. Music, and specifically liturgical and religious music, has indeed become an integral component of this process.

During 1982, the Instituto Nacional Hispano de Liturgia Hispana undertook the study of the structure of the Mass among representative Hispanic communities in the United States. The Bishops' Committee on the Liturgy (BCL [now the USCCB Committee on Divine Worship]) had commissioned this study and challenged the Instituto, in collaboration with the Federation of Diocesan Liturgical Commissions (FDLC), to assess the range of Hispanic responses to current liturgical reforms. The project began on the eve of the twentieth anniversary of Second Vatican Council's promulgation of *Sacrosanctum Concilium*.

While the process used for the study, which polled a random sample of over six hundred Hispanics of Mexican-American, Puerto Rican, Cuban, and other backgrounds, has been published in various periodicals, the results that emerged continue to shape the agenda of the Instituto board meetings and that of other pastoral organizations committed to Hispanic ministry in the country.

Almost unanimously, the study's participants made liturgical music their first priority. Hispanic assemblies continue to make music their most important avenue of expression in worship today. Melody, rhythm, and lyrics blend to provide communitarian expression to a people whose religious roots are universal and, at the same time, imbued with specific life experiences. In and through the musical expression of Hispanic Catholics, the hope of this pilgrim people displays both the suffering and the joy of Jesus and his Church.

SPANISH LITURGICAL MUSIC IN HISPANIC WORSHIP

In the context of our current reflection, we must consider the variety of Hispanic assemblies of our country. Additionally, we reflect on how they display, through their repertoire, both the aesthetic and textual strengths of their compositions, as well as the differences in rhythms and styles that characterize them.

PASTORAL OBSERVATIONS

1. There is a markedly different style of Church experience, and thus Church music, between the eastern seaboard of the United States and the West. The original division provided by the Office of Hispanic Affairs of the Bishops' Conference established eight different regions. While members selected from each region compose the Instituto's board and have served the bishops of those regions in implementing the liturgical reform among Hispanic Catholics, they also promote avenues of inculturation with Hispanic assemblies

2. The liturgical music of each region has been used at national conventions sponsored by the Instituto, as well as at the Spanish tracks sponsored by the National Association of Pastoral Musicians at their regional and national conventions. Hispanic Catholics from all regions have learned to sing and pray with one another

3. Musically, the western section of the United States seems to display a definite Mexican rhythm, which naturally extends from California through Texas and into the Midwest. Exception must be made to a New Mexican, or Southwestern, style of music that points to Spain and its Spanish missionaries as the root of their musical expression

4. The eastern section of the United States seems to experience a strong Caribbean domination in the musical styles used at worship, due primarily to the cultural and religious experience of Catholics from Puerto Rico and the Dominican Republic in the Northeast, and those from Cuba in the Southeast. In the future, this distinction between East and West may not be so marked due to the influx of Mexican and Central American migrants in areas of the Northeast (New York) and the Southeast (the Carolinas and Georgia)

5. During the first decades of the liturgical reform after Vatican II, the music of Spain seemed to have influenced the worship experience of all of these communities, but original music composed by local musicians seems to surface more frequently today as the reform has begun to affect Hispanic Catholic assemblies at prayer. This evolutionary process does not mean to exclude all liturgical music from Spain but, rather, motivate Hispanic Catholics in the United States to see music as the symbol that speaks to and from their hearts and their integrated cultural experience at the center of their intangibles

6. Despite what some non-Hispanic individuals may think or feel as they observe the cultural experience of Hispanics from the outward circumference of tangibles, neither the Spanish language nor worshipping in Spanish is a problem for Hispanic Catholics in this country. However, we must all admit that there exists, among the Hispanic regions, a variety of language nuances in the use of Spanish and definite preferences of musical styles. We discover this same variety and these preferences, of course, in the regionalism of most of the countries of the world

7. In summary, for anyone to address this topic, a diverse repertoire must always be presented to include selections from the following areas that represent diverse assemblies: New Mexico, Texas, California, the Northwest, the Northeast, and the Southeast of the United States; sub-culturally speaking, from Spanish-Mexico, Tex-Mex (Texas-Mexican), the Californian sound, the Northwestern sound, Puerto Rico, the Dominican Republic, and Cuba. Our contention is always the same in each case: the liturgical music of these assemblies reflects not only the unique Church experience of those who worship in that area, but also a longing to sing with one another as a pilgrim community bound by a common origin and a common purpose in Christ.

CONCLUDING REMARKS

As we have listened to these selections, I venture to offer these conclusions that are only my personal perception of the state of Hispanic liturgical music in the United States:

1. We have finally moved from the exclusive use of liturgical music from Spain to the composition, publication, and interpretation of music composed in Spanish-speaking countries outside of the United States and of music composed by Hispanic composers in the United States. Several things have contributed to this change:

   a. The increased awareness of Hispanic heritage as a gift and not as a threat to North American society (as described in the pastoral letter of our bishops several years ago and witnessed to by the various Encuentros Nacionales of the past two decades)

   b. The increased participation of Hispanic communities in parishes and dioceses throughout the country and the revolutionary impact that the discovery of the Scriptures have brought about in individual Catholics after the Second Vatican Council

    c. The increased commitment of national organizations and regional corporations to the publication of Hispanic liturgical materials and the associated financial risks incurred to serve our Hispanic assemblies. In addition to the Instituto Nacional Hispano de Liturgia, they are Benziger (now RCL Benziger), Oregon Catholic Press (OCP), Liturgy Training Publications (LTP), and World Library Publications (WLP)

2. These local compositions reflect the different ecclesial realities that constitute the assemblies that sing them:

    a. Many of our Hispanic Catholics, with the new wave of immigration of the last thirty years, find in the rhythms of their country of origin (as well as in the religious festivals that provide the framework for this music) an avenue of social adaptation in a new setting that, different from their own, causes multiple strains on their religious experience. Music, as a symbol, assists them to experience the healing touch of their heritage and allows them to move forward in their process of integration to North American society

    b. Most of our Hispanic Catholics who have already dwelled in North American territory for centuries (mostly in the western and southwestern regions) enjoy the music of their country of origin, namely Mexico or, in some cases, the countries of Central America. Perhaps this is because it echoes the joyful heritage from which they came rather than the need for social adaptation in the present. While this assertion appears to be true, many families strongly fear that most of their youngsters tend to reject their Hispanic heritage and feel disoriented and confused. Yet Hispanic traditions seem to remain through music (e.g., young Mariachi groups frequently surface)

    c. Even so, one cannot speak of Hispanic Catholic liturgy or the musical experience in the United States in a uniform manner. Though one people, united by a common language and tradition, their assemblies express their faith in slightly different ways as they bring a variety of ecclesial realities to the liturgy of the Church. One of these realities, ever-present in the Southwest, is that of bilingual celebrations

3. Some claim bilingual music provides the answer for Hispanic Catholics in the United States. Although the concept is not unique to this country and even to the Church, current efforts fail to grasp the uniqueness

of the concept. What we hear now—and unfortunately what some assemblies have embraced without any constructive critique—may be described as Spanish texts fitted into North American musical modes or styles, which speak to the heart of North Americans sensitive to Hispanic ministry and to some bilingual communities, but not to all.

a. Composers must take care in the use of the Spanish language in music, particularly the consistency and balance of the Spanish accent with the musical accents of the melodies they create

b. To become an authentic expression of the assembly, bilingual music needs to emerge from the theological, social, and liturgical reflection of bilingual or multicultural community. A local choice must be made whether community members will make an effort to sing one another's language and musical styles or combine them in a creative manner

c. The current repertoire of bilingual or multilingual texts function better as verses of an antiphonal composition that maintains a dominant language in its antiphons, as is the style of many Taizé pieces

4. Hispanic Catholics enjoy praying and singing in the musical styles of other cultural groups that constitute the Church of the United States. They find no difficulty in being part of the mosaic of cultures and joining in the rich tradition of hymnody in many Anglo assemblies and the moving rhythmical spirituals of African American communities. I feel they are even open to learn more about the Asian population that is growing considerably, especially in California, Texas, Louisiana, and New York.

Can others come to know Hispanic Catholics through our liturgical music? Will they sing with us the hope-filled songs of a new life without oppression, prejudice, or resentment? Our Church and our faith provide the framework for such hope. As this hope becomes a reality in all Catholic assemblies of the United States, the Kingdom of Jesus Christ will become more evident to all.

CATECHISTS FOR THE NEW MILLENNIUM
A reflection for those who are called to translate the power of the word to the lives of God's people in the third millennium

I presented this keynote reflection to the Catechetical Congress of the Diocese of Browns-ville, Texas, on Sunday, September 9, 2001. They invited me to stay longer in the diocese and to journey to Mexico, practically next door. I almost stayed until Tuesday, but decided to return home on Monday, the day before the infamous attacks of 9/11 that changed our world.

I feel privileged to be with you today, among so many dedicated lay leaders of our Church, teachers and preachers in their own right, bearers of the message of Jesus Christ, our Lord and, thus, committed disciples of his Kingdom. Our task as catechists may seem arduous for some but, with God's help, it becomes easier each year as we grow and mature spiritually by drawing closer to the Lord and his Church while being faithful to his mission.

Our reflections today, moreover, lead us to consider our mission as catechists in the new millennium, that is to say, in the present and in the future of our Church. Let us tackle it, then, by attempting to respond to four questions that are basic to anyone who is discerning a commitment:
- Who are these catechists?
- What do they do?
- To whom do they do what they do?
- How do they do it?

I hope that you are not confused about these questions. No, our task today is not to get confused about our mission but, hopefully, to become clearer about our role in the Church and to celebrate it during this wonderful day in the diocese of Brownsville with the focus "With Love beyond All Telling." Although the answers to these four basic questions may overlap a bit, if after this presentation you are still a bit confused, I give you permission to tell me; then, I will bite my tongue and understand that you want to help other audiences in the future by keeping my mouth shut.

WHO ARE THESE CATECHISTS?
As catechists, we are translators not of any spoken language, but of the truths about Christ and his Church, translators of concepts and feelings, of images revealed to us by the Word-Made-Flesh and alive in the community, translators of a precious message. Just as theologians help us reflect upon the mystery of God in our lives, just as musicians transform the texts of the Church into poetry and

melodies that sing the praises of God, we, as catechists, stand before people who are hungry for spiritual meaning in their lives. They are at times confused about their origin and their purpose, people who expect us to lead their children, their youngsters, and even themselves, to a spiritual path with meaning. Our calling is to translate the presence of God, who walks among them as a pilgrim, but whom they cannot seem to name or find. We must show them the way to the God who calls them to live with him forever!

As catechists, we stand in awe before that presence, revealed in word and sacrament, to guide us through our journey of life, and we profess a creed at Sunday worship that summarizes for us and for others the story of this revelation. As catechists, we stand in a world with many options, committed to help others to remember the option that was made at their baptism: the way of Jesus. It is a way of discipleship, compassion, and forgiveness, but also a way that engages the individual in making choices. These choices come from a formed conscience and not from ideas acquired through rugged individualism or the relativism that prevails in our society in this new millennium. As catechists, we attempt to carry out this mission using all of our senses, not only emphasizing the need to memorize the truths of our faith, but also appealing to the heart of those who want to know Jesus, thereby relating catechesis to liturgy, to social justice and, ultimately, to all life.

At times, we seem to forget that, although we accept this mission, God ultimately has the last word on it. Let us not burn bridges but, rather, build them. As good translators of God's good news, I urge you not to see problems in your mission but, rather, possibilities! Parents who drop off their children at our parish facilities are not a problem but a possibility; they may be fertile soil in need of the good seed of the Gospel, and not necessarily a soil that will choke it off. Do not get frustrated and, above all, do not show your frustration to the children or to the parents. Do the best you can with those children and sow the seed of the Gospel within them. Let God take care of their parents through them. Be a bridge, a mediator, an instrument, a translator of God's word into the everyday language of life.

What Are We Actually Translating?

As catechists, we are bound to translate who Jesus is for us by living out his way ourselves, as we teach it to others. We should reflect on who Jesus is for us. Is Jesus a concept, an idea, or an image? Each day we must ask ourselves: "How real is Jesus to me? How close am I to him? Am I aware that I am the bridge that brings unto others the awareness of resurrected life, and that I can only do this if I accept my own cross as he accepted his?" I don't have to inflict pain on myself and enjoy it. I am not called to be a masochist. However, life is not perfect, to say the least, and it presents us options that at times require our own pain so that others can live and enjoy it. At times, this pain translates itself into challenges and responsibilities that our human nature alone does not want to accept. Nevertheless, with God's strength we must accept them: raising our children at home while putting aside our careers, working two jobs to pay for our studies, leaving home and security to begin a new life for the sake of our families, and taking risks that don't always work out. Are we willing to translate the meaning of the cross, the victory of Jesus' Paschal Mystery, resurrected life, to those entrusted to our care in the catechetical ministry of the Church?

If we search deeply into our own life experiences, I am sure that we can find stories of redemption where the Paschal Mystery of Jesus Christ has become evident. Such a story is a contemporary reflection of the resurrection. At some point in our catechetical ministry, let us find the courage to tell that story to others, for we are called to tell the story of Jesus himself in words and languages and images that can not only capture the imaginations of our people, but also their hearts. Our calling as catechists is to translate the mystery of God's beauty in the midst of the pains and aches of contemporary society in this third millennium. We are agents and ambassadors of Christ to the world around us.

TO WHOM DO WE TRANSLATE THE MYSTERY OF JESUS?

Simply put, we translate it to a society filled with many options in which materialism, relativism, and rapid social changes prevail. What a challenge for the Church!

Like those entrusted to our care, we are drawn to the materialism of our newspaper ads and the television commercials that promise us how to look more beautiful, thin, and appealing to one another. Despite the difficulties with the economy today, we are still drawn to buying and spending, to consuming, to accumulating treasures, and not to sharing too much with others.

We are drawn to a way of thinking that permits any behavior that pleases us at any time. It proclaims "Whatever I think or feel as right is right." It is a way of thinking that centers around the person who needs no God or who at times searches for a God who is far away and distant, everywhere and yet not historical, a God who is not personal and who cannot make me commit myself to anyone or to anything, unless I want to.

This way of thinking gives more importance to psychics and visionaries who make lots of money on television than the guidance of Church leaders. Pope John Paul II has called this global outlook of contemporary society the "culture of death." I respectfully call it a "culture of disposables." As we dispose of diapers, paper goods, and old clothes, we are learning how to dispose of God's most precious creation—the human person—whether that person is unborn, disabled, or even punished by society to die.

As a society and as Catholics, we are faced with this way of thinking and being, we are called to translate the power of Christ's resurrection, the mystery of his cross, the meaning of sacrifice and the hope of eternal life as we share in a communion of love that is not to be broken. What an awesome task! And you thought the Roman Circus and the Coliseum were tough!

Remember that you are not alone, so do not get discouraged. Jesus is with us until the end, as Saint Paul has written in his Letter to the Romans (8:35): "Who can separate us from the love of Christ?" This is our challenge! Some people are seduced by demons who claim personal enjoyments are so necessary and that anything else about heaven can wait for later in life. Heaven cannot wait, nor can it be substituted by material goods or addictive pleasures. The kingdom of God is in our midst and we need to help others live the enjoyable signs of that kingdom now and later.

HOW ARE WE TO CARRY OUT THIS MISSION?

Do you remember the second reading at Mass from the letter to the Hebrews (Twenty-Second Sunday in Ordinary Time, Year C)? The author wanted to answer this question with many words, as if attempting to unravel a mystery that cannot be deciphered in one paragraph, but he tried as he wrote:

> ...you have not drawn near to an untouchable mountain and a blazing
> fire, nor gloomy darkness and storm and trumpet blast, nor a voice
> speaking words such that those who heard begged that they be not
> addressed to them.....No, you have drawn near to Mount Zion and
> the city of the living God, the heavenly Jerusalem, to myriads of angels
> in festal gathering, to the assembly of the firstborn enrolled in heaven,
> and God the judge of all, to the spirits of just men made perfect, to Jesus,
> the mediator of a new covenant, and the sprinkled blood which speaks
> more eloquently than that of Abel.... (Hebrews 12:18–19, 22–24a)

Jesus is the mediator of a new covenant, the true bridge and path between God and humanity, the way, the truth, and the life. Can there be any doubt? Of course not! When we reflect upon how we are to bring this awareness to others, we confront a double task: to know him and to know ourselves as well. The closer we come to know him, the more we discover the richness of our humanity, destined for a glorious transformation, for he chose to become one like us in all things but sin and his victory over death is ours to cherish for all times. This gift we call redemption is a gift accessible to all humanity. The closer we come to know ourselves, the more we discover the possibilities of becoming what he wants us to become, namely, fully human and capable of redemption. The full awareness of ourselves as being fully human leads us to empty ourselves out for others as Jesus did!

In liturgy we call this double process the Paschal Mystery, and we celebrate it in every sacrament, but especially at the Eucharist. As we approach his banquet of love on earth, we are called to become more human each day so that we may one day participate in the divinity that Jesus has provided for us at the heavenly banquet. We do it by dying and rising with him each day of our lives, by being honest to ourselves and authentic in our faith.

"How do we carry out this mission?" we ask ourselves. Not with arrogance, but as the topic of your Congress today expresses it "With love beyond all telling." Like Jesus is to us the mediator of a new covenant, we are to become the translators of that new covenant of love and compassion to those entrusted to our care.

CONCLUSION

I once read about an educator who was asked "What qualities characterize an ideal teacher?" This was the answer given:
- Must be enthusiastic
- Must teach with joy
- Must show great interest in the students and be committed to their growth
- Must know what he or she teaches and so must motivate the students in the subject matter which in his/her passionate way is communicated
- Must relate well to those entrusted to his/her care

Unknown to this educator, the characteristics of an ideal teacher were captured by the four Evangelists. Each of them preached and collected the story of Jesus. Christ showed this enthusiasm and joy, this interest for others so much that he motivated them to come to know the Father as he taught them through parables and stories that broke through the mere fulfillment of laws and precepts. He healed the sick and comforted the sorrowing. He fished with the Apostles and prepared dinner for the crowd. He cast out demons and read the Scriptures at synagogue services. He ultimately carried the cross in his obedience to his Father.

Jesus, indeed, is the mediator of a new covenant, as the preface of the second Sunday of Advent reminds us: "His future coming was proclaimed by all the prophets. The virgin mother bore him in the womb with love beyond all telling. John the Baptist was his herald and made him known when at last he came." Well, he comes to us each day and we are the bearers of his message. How joyful, how awesome it is to be the catechists of this third millennium and to translate the power of his life in the midst of darkness and distress! Hang in there, dear catechists. May God bless you in your mission!

HISPANIC PASTORAL MUSICIANS:
OF THE CHURCH, IN THE CHURCH, FOR THE CHURCH

A reflection on the role of liturgy and music
in the Hispanic Catholic assemblies of the US

The following essay was delivered as a keynote presentation at the first gathering of Hispanic Pastoral Musicians in Albuquerque, New Mexico, on April 11, 1999. Most of the conclusions in this essay have been taken from my bilingual talk "La Espiritualidad en el Ministerio de la Música" at the Hispanic Pastoral Musicians Conference in Las Cruces, New Mexico, on July 24–27, 2003.

It is indeed a pleasure for me to share with you some of my reflections at this important conference that aims to cover so many topics here in Albuquerque. Many are the overall titles that are proposed for our consideration during these days:

- Celebrating our faith in the Lord
- The third millennium
- Pastoral musicians as artisans and united in Christ for the Church of the future

I know that the coordinators of this conference have tried to meet the many needs of our Hispanic pastoral musicians. They have to assemble these presentations with urgency because the topics affect us all. The conference leaders are striving to prepare us for our liturgical ministry and, united by the same calling, to help us serve our assemblies in the name of Jesus. May each of us respond to the needs of Christ's Church with enthusiasm and joy. Allow me, then, to congratulate the members of the coordinating committee of this conference for their persistence in bringing about this vital gathering with interest and adept organization. I congratulate them for sharing their gifts with us and inspiring us to share our gifts with others. I also hope this conference will animate us to share whatever we learn or experience during the next few days with those who could not attend; I suspect they are the most needy among us.

For my part, I will first address the place of our pastoral ministry within the ecclesial community that experienced the power of the Spirit on Pentecost Sunday through the preaching of the apostles. This community heard the message of the Gospel in the plurality and diversity of all those who were listening: the Church. I cannot believe that the apostles only preached the Gospel with words; I trust that the Spirit gave them strength to sing out new melodies that proclaimed a new dawn for the world. They did so within the context of their Jewish religious culture, so accustomed to praising God in words, songs, gestures, and even dancing, namely, with their whole body.

Indeed, this is one of the descriptions of this early Christian community given to us in the Acts of the Apostles, chapter 4. In the midst of an oppressive society—as the Roman Empire was—the early Christians learned how to live their faith, share their goods and their gifts with others, and surrender their lives for Jesus. This was 2,000 years ago. What has happened to us since then? If today's Christians have forgotten to live like the Christians of the Scriptures, perhaps our mission as pastoral musicians may be to help. Through our service, we can remind Christ's followers how to believe and to celebrate the Good News of Jesus with excitement and conviction within the context of our contemporary society that Pope John Paul II called, in *Tertio Millennio Adveniente*, "the culture of death."

We need to recall, though briefly, what this phrase is all about because we are involved in it indeed. Families continue to disintegrate and the decisions we seem to make as adults are often made away from the love of God and neighbor, our most significant commandment. The various means of communication seduce us to live individual and private lives; in fact, they invite us to consume more products that will make us thinner, prettier and younger, products that will help us achieve success in life. We see television commercials addressing themselves to the exterior part of our being but hardly any touch upon the necessary means each of us must pursue to cultivate the interior part of our self, our soul, our heart.

Moreover, we have all witnessed how many of society's criteria appear to have filtered through the ranks of the Church. Financial cuts and downsizing, though I am sure necessary in many dioceses and parishes, have given the impression that we can easily do without as many people, that we don't need them at all. This may be so in some cases. What our lay people question is the way these issues have been handled. This impression, though not intended by the Church decision makers, appears contrary to the New Testament value that presents the Church as the body of Christ in which each member has unique gifts to contribute to the whole community. At the opposite side of the spectrum, we know of some who feel they are indispensable or untouchable.

The "culture of death"[1] affects us all in many ways. Many of us live lives where we abandon children or ignore the elderly because they are not young, pretty, or thin. This culture of death invites us to believe in a cosmic God who is everywhere and yet nowhere. It speaks of a God who is not a person and who has no place in history; he is the God of the New Age, the God of multiple religious movements and confused syncretisms. It is a topic that I describe in my Spanish publication, *Sectas, Cultos y Sincretismos*.[2] Faced with this culture of death, we need to stand together as Church.

The Church, the *ekklesia*, the gathering of believers and witnesses of Jesus Christ, invites us to profess one faith in a personal and historical God who journeys with us and dwells among us. The Church challenges us to preach, with our own voices, melodies, and rhythms, the message of salvation to a pluralistic and diverse assembly. Called by Jesus—and each of us oriented to grow in him—together we become Church, and in the Church and for the Church (though not exclusively) does our ministry exist and develop.

The point remains clear: as ministers of the Church we need to rely on our spirituality as we are affected by our own arrogance, by a decision-making process that emerges out of financial constraints and does not include other criteria, or by the social pressures of contemporary society.

I propose that our service within the Church and for the Church should reflect three different, though essential, ingredients:

- It is a service to the *word of God* and not to our subjective or individual words
- It is a service that involves *a personal commitment to the community* and not to our own individual self-interests
- It is a service that *engages us totally in a faith experience, a gift from God who demands that we live as signs of Christ's resurrection/liberation for others*

Ours is a calling, as pastoral musicians, to become witnesses of the Lord in the community, agents of a new evangelization that is committed to free the poor from their poverty so that they may experience, through us, the authentic love of God. Let us develop these three ingredients as the heart and center of our reflections. I share them with you from my own personal context as an amateur musician and not as a priest or a pastor. I served in the role of musician and music director at the seminary years before I was ordained a priest!

PASTORAL MUSICIANS SERVICE GOD'S WORD

The word of God illumines our existence and gives meaning to our pilgrimage on this earth through this culture of death. Without the revealed word, our learned words would have no meaning. When we tell our children, our spouses, our significant others, our intimate friends that we love them, we do it freely because we have felt loved first, because we dare believe and celebrate the fact that God has loved us first in Jesus Christ.

When we choose songs for the liturgy or for any of our sacraments, when we compose antiphons for the assembly, when we recommend new melodies to help us all deepen our faith, as pastoral musicians, our priority lies in the analyses we make of the texts. These lyrics, the words that appear in these songs, should be based primarily on the word of God and not be exclusively of our own invention.

As pastoral musicians, we must be apart from the many popular composers and singers who proclaim love through their songs, often in a tragic manner expressing in their boleros or ballads the frustrations of those who can no longer live as one, or the many others who search for someone to love or someone to love them! Their songs sound a bit like the stories of televised *novelas* (soap operas) that announce the same stories, the same anguish, and almost the identical tragedies in multiple ways. How different is the story of Christians, always enriched by promises of peace and hope!

Although the reforms of the Second Vatican Council opened the way for us to inculturate or adapt our local rhythms, the depth of culture reflected in our compositions can be born neither out of moments of frustration nor images of pessimism. We can ask ourselves, "Where are we to find these images?" The answers become clearer as we grow in love of the Church and in the word of God, a word that announces life and hope for those who long to fulfill their covenant with the Lord and for those who already celebrate its coming in Jesus.

It is in the poetic structure of the psalms and in the images of the Gospel that we find sufficient materials to compose, choose, and sing out the praises of our God in the midst of our deficient cultural surroundings. Our words alone, I propose, are poor before God, who calls us and sends us forth to become his ministers. Our words will improve as we deepen our own spirituality in the Word-Made-Flesh and as we place ourselves at his service. We must begin by engaging ourselves deeply in the meaning of the word. How important it is for all of our musicians—composers, choir members, instrumentalists, and leaders of song—to grow in the knowledge and love of the Scriptures by attending Bible courses that may help them deepen the word in our own personal experiences.

PASTORAL MUSICIANS ARE COMMITTED TO THE ASSEMBLY AND NOT TO THEIR OWN SELF-INTERESTS

Since the Church "opened its windows,"[3] in 1963 we continue to grow in the reforms of the Second Vatican Council. It is worth noting that the *Constitution on the Sacred Liturgy*, signed by the Council fathers as their first document, has provided us with five general criteria by which our pastoral and liturgical ministry should be guided:

1. Participation of the assembly in worship that leads to the other criteria
2. The use of the vernacular language
3. The rediscovery of the word of God
4. The development of liturgical ministries among the laity
5. Cultural adaptation, known in theological and liturgical circles as "inculturation"

We are empowered by the fourth criterion, the development of ministries, as we strive to serve the Church as pastoral musicians. Precisely because we stand together as children of the same God, and as brothers and sisters in the same Lord, we live in and for the Church and feel with the Church as if we were listening to two distinct bells. On one side, we hear a bell that resounds with the gong of the universal community of faith; on the other, we hear a bell that echoes the needs and hopes of our local Church community. In the balance, we share our healthy, creative juices as we recognize that the liturgy of our assemblies reflects the ecclesiology of its members.

At times, we feel the brunt of such tension in the way we are asked to choose music. It is through the music that we sing, and through the words that support such melodies that we measure the theological thermometer of the community that gathers to pray. It is significant for us to grow theologically with the Church and to help others grow theologically; our musical repertoire should reflect such growth!

How do we do this? Already in the English translation of our bishops' *Music in Catholic Worship* and *Liturgical Music Today*,[4] both published in Spanish by the Instituto Nacional Hispano de Liturgia, we discover the principles that will help us choose and share the best possible repertoire in and for our assemblies. The documents speak of musical judgment, liturgical judgment, and pastoral judgment. As for musical judgment, we might ask, "Is this song singable? Is it accessible to the whole assembly and not just to choir members?" Liturgical judgment implores, "Where in the liturgy does it best fit, in which rite, and at what ritual moment? Is it good for a funeral or a baptism or a wedding?" Pastoral judgment asks, "Is this community ready for this song? If I know my assembly well, what am I risking when I introduce a somewhat controversial piece?" For pastoral judgment to be effective, I must add that the input of an entire liturgical committee should be sought.

Although we understood the seriousness of our service, and we have grown in the ministry to which we are called, we may not know when or how we were called. Once we have stepped forward to help others meet Jesus in prayer through music, then we will be able to surrender our musical talents to the Church, leaving aside many of our self-interests. Are we motivated by the love of Jesus whose Spirit animates our work as a labor of love for the Church? In reality, the answer to this question and to many others becomes clearer if we have embraced what I call a true liturgical spirituality.

Liturgical spirituality includes the knowledge of the liturgy of the Church as it was before the Council, as it is now, and as it might be in the future. We always keep in mind that Jesus, through the leadership of the Church, cares for our pilgrim community and orders all things for the good of all. Liturgical spirituality includes letting go of personal interests and moving aside for the sake of worship. Liturgical spirituality engages the disciple of Jesus in an act of giving more than taking or receiving. Liturgical spirituality requires us to know liturgy well and to grow in the knowledge of liturgy to complement the love we have for it already.

This liturgical spirituality of our musicians is quite inclusive; it engages us as pastoral musicians to become active ministers of a Church that is community, institution, and servant of God. Ours is a Church that collaborates with others in the mission of bringing the Gospel of Jesus to the lives of those who do not know it. Ours is a Church that keeps order and is willing to work together for the good of all. We serve a Church that inspires us to drop our instruments and silence our voices that we might bring the good news of Jesus to the homeless, the prisoners, and the oppressed.

OUR MINISTRY IS A TRUE FAITH RESPONSE: TRANSFORMED AND TRANSFORMING

Our liturgical life demands that we carry out the same actions as Jesus in his ministry. The movement of our Christian calling goes from prayer into action. We are also called to live this ministry outside of the worship or prayer experience of the Church. We are to take our minstry into the marketplace. It is not enough to compose or to sing prophetic songs. If we are to be faithful to the new evangelization to which all of us are called, our community must see that we live in accord with such prophetic texts.

Being transformed by the power of the Spirit and helping in the transformation of others through our ministry is an awesome task! Spirituality makes us aware that we never accomplish all that we intended to do. It helps us to realize that there is always much more to be done, and that that it may not all be done by us. Rather, it is those whom we have inspired that continue the work or the mission that we are embracing today. We are not running this ministry! The Lord is running it, whether we like it or not. Moreover, at times, the Lord has a great sense of humor that catches us by surprise.

If we live a double life, what the Gospel describes as hypocritical may also describe us. The disciples, when Jesus spoke about the Pharisees, heeded his warning clearly: "Do what they say, but do not imitate what they do," for what they do and what they say is not the same.[5] Pastoral musicians who do not live in communion with their community and, therefore, with other ministers of the community, may fall victim to three temptations that I refer to as musical demons:

- The demon of demanding urges: things have to be done my way because I am the leader

- The demon of competing: whatever we do here is much better than whatever is done there
- The demon of self-sufficiency: I do not need anyone's help and I do not need to attend any more courses or share any more with anyone
- Let us accumulate the gifts that we already have
- They need us; we do not need them.

What can we do to free ourselves from such demons? We must live in communion with others at prayer. We must experience prayer and not merely lead prayers for others. Even though we are committed to help and nurture others, how can we be nurtured in the Lord? We have to cultivate an active life of prayer that can help us grow in our communion with others. We must not think we can make it alone, especially if we want to go beyond ourselves into assisting the needs of the anawim, the most needy among us.

Private and communal prayer will help us exorcise the demon of demanding so that we can grow in the sharing of our talents with others. A life of prayer helps free us of the demon of competing so that we can collaborate in the building of the Kingdom with others. As we conquer the demon of self-sufficiency, we can experience the fellowship of being Church, and we truly become aware it is together, not alone, that we are called to journey to that eternal happiness promised to all.

As a result of our God-given gift of faith, our response grows out of our own commitment toward those who Jesus places before us. We cannot turn our eyes from the features of the Lord in faces of the poorest and most needy among us; we cannot stop singing songs of hope and commitment that may animate their existence and, hopefully, change it.

CONCLUSION

I proposed three basic ingredients for the spirituality of the Hispanic pastoral musicians (and for any musicians) in our twenty-first century. I speak to the choir directors, instrumentalists, choir members, organists, and guitarists. I propose a BLT spirituality! These are the three ingredients, the bacon, lettuce and tomato, of this Church's musical minister: biblical, liturgical and transforming. While I hope this acronym does not become a popular cliché or a slogan, it does capture how our spiritual lives must grow and mature in the service of the Lord and his community. We grow in biblical knowledge, liturgical sensitivity, and transformative faith-filled spirit.

Ours is a journey of faith that takes us from the experience of Christ to the experience of his Church. We go from the Church to the world that needs to see our personal and communal witnessing to faith. This is our challenge as we face the threshold of the third millennium.

Maybe some of us may perceive that they cannot carry out all that the Church expects of them as pastoral musicians. Fear not, do not lose hope, and trust in the Lord. He has promised to be with us always and to guide us through our ministry. If we live in a continuous dialogue with him through prayer and in the spirit of collaboration, there is nothing to fear.

When we place ourselves at the service of his word and not to our own whims, we will be better committed to the community serve. As we offer them our talent to help them grow, we will also grow with them. We attend to the needs of the most needy around us as a response to the gift of faith that we have received.

In conclusion, we become instruments and not obstacles of the Risen Lord. We share our faith in a world that needs to hear his story and to celebrate his life with new melodies and new rhythms.

---

[1] The term was used extensively by Pope John II in *Tertio Millennio Adveniente* (1994).

[2] Sosa, Juan J. *Sectas, Cultos y Sincretismos* (Miami, FL: Ediciones Universal, 1999).

[3] A popular expression attributed the calling of the Second Vatican Council by Pope John XXIII.

[4] The original translations into Spanish of these documents are in *Los Documentos Litúrgicos* (Chicago: Liturgy Training Publications, 1997). After extensive review with much input from clergy and laity, these documents were supplanted by *Sing to the Lord: Music in Divine Worship* (USCCB: November 2007).

[5] The Gospel of Mark presents us various examples of the tension between Jesus and the Pharisees; one example is in Mark 7:1–13.

CONCLUSION

Since I first presented these reflections, other documents have been issued to guide the liturgical life of our bishops, our parishes, our communities, and the people of God. The Vatican issued a new edition of the *General Instruction of the Roman Missal* and *Liturgicam Authenticam*, the fifth instruction on the vernacular translation of the Roman liturgy in 2001; *Redemptionis Sacramentum* was issued in 2004. Each of these texts indicates that the work of the Second Vatican Councils mandated for reform has not ended. The dialogue on liturgical praxis and liturgical theology, held at high academic levels, continues to echo the discussions of the Council fathers on the eve of December 4, 1963, when the *Constitution on the Sacred Liturgy* (*Sacrosanctum Concilium*) was promulgated.

The pastoral dialogue on the major criterion of the liturgical reform (i.e., participation by all who worship) continues in our local dioceses and parish communities. From an ecclesial perspective, this dialogue is shaped by:

- The spirituality of our lay ministers and the liturgical formation of our seminaries
- The ongoing dialogue among both a sense of the sacred and an exalted experience of community worship
- Good music and not-so-good texts
- Popular piety and liturgical celebrations
- A dialogue between theologians and celebrations that shapes the vision of those who celebrate the Paschal Mystery together

I am delighted to see this dialogue among the many cultures that shape the multicultural reality of this nation. Perhaps this phenomenon in the United States will bring a continued dialogue about faith and culture, as it began to take place during the last decades of the twentieth century. The exploration of a true, authentic inculturation, however, cannot take place unless the local communities accept one another as a communion of believers. The first step is their acceptance of the reality that together they constitute a mosaic of cultures. Many writers will address this topic in the future, for it lies at the heart of a process of evangelization that echoes the call of Jesus and of the Church to save all and to lose none.

While many more essays and conference presentations will address the multicultural reality of our Church, allow me to share a simple story. It is a personal experience that summarizes it for me and, hopefully, for you.

From time to time, there is a privilege handed down to priests who exercise their ministry in Florida. They are selected to be chaplains of one of the many cruise lines that set sail from Miami and Ft. Lauderdale. On this particular occasion, I was privileged to be the chaplain on a two-week cruise that included Venezuela. On our second stop in Venezuela, I decided to spend a day with a priest-friend who lived in Caracas. After a wonderful day's journey, he took me back to the port of La Guaira to join the ship on its return trip to San Juan, Puerto Rico. I stepped out of his car, we said goodbye, and I walked to the pier from which the ship was to depart. As I approached the pier slowly, I noticed that the ship was not there; it was actually closer to the horizon than to the pier. The ship had departed. What can Father do? There I stood with my camera, my wallet with one credit card, no passport, and only $25.00 cash.

I sought help in the nearest Catholic church, the only one in town. After much talk to convince the pastor, he let me sleep there that night and tried to call a friend to arrange my legal exit from Venezuela the following day. Thank God this all happened before 9/11!

I slept that night in what we may consider primitive conditions. On the following morning, the only permanent deacon of the diocese, who happened to be a taxi driver, drove me to the Maiquetía airport, where the pastor's contact was supposed to approve my departure. The cab fare was $20.00. I paid for the airfare with the only credit card I had at the time. Before I boarded the plane to San Juan, I made a phone call to Puerto Rico to request another friend's help to pick me up and take me to the ship, which was already there. When I called, no one was home. Had I completed the call, it would have cost $5.00, the only money that I had left. I didn't know it at the time, but $5.00 was the exact amount I needed to pay as the customary Venezuelan departure tax. When I was ready to depart, an officer requested it and needed to see it attached to the boarding pass. I finally completed the procedures and was left with a few quarters for my international flight.

I was so happy to leave Venezuela and arrive in Puerto Rico with enough spare change to make a phone call to my friend, who had since come home and was most helpful to me in my need. He welcomed me into his home, fed me, and took me to the ship the following morning to pick up my luggage from the ship. When I arrived, no one from the cruise line cared to know what had happened.

I had been stranded, undocumented, at the mercy of others, dependent upon Mother Church, and desperately hoping to come through without much anxiety or disgust, and I did! Not at the time, but later, I concluded that God undoubtedly has a sense of humor that only he understands. Moreover, when he laughs at me, he does it with a desire to teach me a lesson.

From that moment on, I cannot ignore anyone who knocks at the door of our parish office or the school, like an abandoned spouse who has no place to go or those whose legal papers are about to expire and who seek legal assistance.

If God has played such tricks on you, do listen to his laughter and let his soothing hand guide you to the love of others. If you ever feel lost and helpless, powerless and dependent, remember to turn to the many faces that surround you, for in and through them you shall find his own.